DATE DUE			

Ernest Hemingway

A Writer's Life

Ernest Hemingway

A Writer's Life

by Catherine Reef

CLARION BOOKS

HOUGHTON MIFFLIN HARCOURT

BOSTON · NEW YORK · 2009

ACKNOWLEDGMENTS

I wish to thank the staff of the John F. Kennedy Presidential Library in Boston for assisting me while carried out the research necessary for this book. Special thanks go to Hemingway curator Susan Wrynn and archives specialist Laurie Austin, as well as to education specialist Sam Rubin, whose 2005 telephone call about another matter led me to write this book on Ernest Hemingway.

Clarion Books • 215 Park Avenue South, New York, NY 10003 • Copyright © 2009 by Catherine Reef • The text was set in 11-point Matt Antique. • All rights reserved.

For information about permission to reproduce selections from this book, write to Permissions, Houghton Mifflin Harcourt Publishing Company, 215 Park Avenue South, New York, NY 10003. • Clarion Books is an imprint of Houghton Mifflin Harcourt Publishing Company. • www.clarionbooks.com • Printed in the United States of America • *Library of Congress Cataloging-in-Publication Data* • Reef. Catherine. Ernest Hemingway: writing from life / Catherine Reef. p. cm. • Includes bibliographical references and index. • ISBN: 978-0-618-98705-4 • 1. Hemingway, Ernest, 1899-1961—Juvenile literature. 2. Authors, American—20th century—Biography—Juvenile literature. I. Title. • PS3515.E37Z754572009 • 813'.52B22 2008032885

MV 10 9 8 7 6 5 4 3 2 1

For Gina Stiassney

CONTENTS

ONE

The Whole World, Boiled Down

In 1923, when he was a young man living in Paris, Ernest Hemingway traveled to Spain to see bullfights. "I was trying to learn to write, commencing with the simplest things, and one of the simplest things of all and the most fundamental is violent death," he said. He thought that the only place to witness violent death, and not feel forced to turn away, was in the bullring.

Twenty-three-year-old Ernest arrived in Pamplona, in northeast Spain, on July 6, with his pregnant wife, Hadley. The tall, athletic Americans stood out among the people filling the Plaza de Toros, the great amphitheater. Ernest had dark hair, brown eyes, a ruddy face, and a stylish mustache. His hearty smile attracted friends the way a pan of fragrant paella draws hungry travelers. Hadley's finest feature was her thick auburn hair, which shone like copper under the Spanish sun.

Around them, men called to the souvenir sellers pushing their way up the aisles, and women waved fans to cool their necks and faces. Then the band let out a loud crash, the crowd cheered, and a colorful procession entered the ring. In marched three *matadors,* the stars of the day's bullfights, wearing tight satin knee breeches and bright capes. They were followed by the *banderilleros,* who would weaken the bulls with gaily

Ernest Hemingway posed for this photograph in Paris in 1922.

decorated barbed wooden sticks, and the *picadors,* who rode on horseback, wielding sharp lances. The matadors bowed before the president's box, and the procession was complete. Assistants unbarred a massive door, and the day's first bull rushed onto the yellow sand.

The first time Ernest saw a bullfight, he expected to hate it. He presumed it would be cruel and empty of meaning. The heavy, powerful bulls were easily angered, quick to charge, and unpredictable, and their sharp horns were lethal. Some matadors had been gored to death in the ring, and others had survived a horn through the hand, belly, or thigh. He also expected to detest the goring of horses, which happened often in the bullring. Stunned horses had been known to trot around the ring dragging their blue entrails, unaware that they were dying.

Yet instead of a dreadful spectacle, he discovered a drama of great beauty, a death struggle raised to an art. He felt no horror on seeing horses killed, and this surprised him. The goring of horses was one small part of a ritual that began with the vibrant entry of the bullfighters and ended, always, with the bull's death.

"The bullfight was so far from simple and I liked it so much," Hemingway said. He became an *aficionado,* or lover, of bullfights, and would return to see them again and again. He was drawn to any pursuit that matched one man's strength and stamina against those of another or against the forces of nature. He loved boxing, hunting, and deep-sea fishing.

He was also drawn to death.

In 1923, when he and Hadley went to Spain, Hemingway had written only short stories and newspaper reports. Three years later, he would publish a novel inspired by the bullfights. This book, *The Sun Also Rises,*

An amateur photographer snapped this picture of bullfighters entering a Spanish bullring around 1918.

Tanned and smiling, Hemingway stands beside a tuna he caught off Bimini, in the Bahamas.

made Ernest Hemingway famous. He followed it with other notable books, among them *A Farewell to Arms,* based on his adventures in World War I; *For Whom the Bell Tolls,* a novel of the Spanish Civil War; and *The Old Man and the Sea,* a novella about one man's refusal to let nature defeat him. He became one of the most famous writers in the world, and in 1954, he was awarded the Nobel Prize for literature.

Hemingway's passions and his impulses influenced what he wrote. His stories reflected what he honestly felt, and not what he had been taught to feel. If he wrote about war, or big-game hunting in Africa, or fighting off sharks at sea, he was describing things that he had done or had seen happen in front of his own eyes. He believed that "[if] a man is making a story up it will be true in proportion to the amount of knowledge of life that he has and how conscientious he is." An author who wrote in this way lived a life filled with risks and adventures, and Hemingway welcomed every test of courage.

Writing was the greatest test of all for Ernest Hemingway. "It is a perpetual challenge and it is more difficult than anything else that I have ever done—so I do it," he wrote in 1935. "And it makes me happy when I do it well."

But a time would come when he no longer did it well, when the right words hovered beyond his reach, and his work fell short of his earlier greatness. Then he would know the deepest despair.

Ernest Hemingway made a lasting impact on the craft of fiction by writing simple sentences and choosing short words rather than long ones. "If I started to write elaborately, or like someone introducing or presenting something, I found that I could cut that scrollwork or ornament and throw it away and start with the first true simple declarative sentence I

While reporting on the Spanish Civil War for U.S. newspapers in 1937 and 1938, Hemingway picked up a gun and fought.

The Swedish ambassador to Cuba presents Ernest Hemingway with the Nobel Prize for literature in 1954.

had written," he explained. Then he would proceed, placing one plain sentence after another.

"There is no flesh whatever to his writing, no softness, no roundness, no color, no flow of muscle under the skin," observed Fanny Butcher, a leading literary critic, in 1929. "There is nothing but uncompromising bone."

This writing style—more like a newspaper reporter's than a novelist's—caused a sensation. For generations, countless young writers tried to sound like Ernest Hemingway. "You can't open a novel or short story in France, or in England or Germany or Italy or anywhere else, without noticing that Hemingway has passed that way," commented Hemingway's friend Sylvia Beach, the famous Paris bookseller.

Hemingway viewed his writing style as a means to an end. He said, "I am trying to make, before I get through, a picture of the whole world— or as much of it as I have seen. Boiling it down always, rather than spreading it out thin."

TWO

"A Fine Big Manly Fellow"

On an early spring day in 1905, five-year-old Ernest Hemingway ran into his grandfather's sickroom to announce, breathlessly, that he had just stopped a breakaway horse—with his own hands, all by himself.

As Ernest raced off to star in his next adventure, his grandfather laughed. "Mark my words," he said, "this boy is going to be heard from some day. If he uses his imagination for good purposes, he'll be famous, but if he starts the wrong way, with all his energy, he'll end in jail."

Grandfather Hall's house, in solidly white, mostly Protestant Oak Park, Illinois, was Ernest Miller Hemingway's first home. He was born there at eight A.M. on July 21, 1899. On that morning, a neighbor named Mrs. Bagley was awakened by loud trumpeting coming from the house behind her own. She shouted to her daughter, "The Hemingways have a boy!" Ernest's father, Dr. Clarence Edmonds Hemingway, had promised to play his cornet on the porch if he had a son.

Ernest's mother had wanted another daughter, though. When Ernest began walking, Grace Hall Hemingway delighted in dressing him and his sister, Marcelline, who was eighteen months older, as twin girls in pink gingham dresses and flowered bonnets. It was common at the start of the twentieth century for very young boys to have long hair and wear dresses,

Ernest Hemingway was born in his grandfather's house, at 439 Oak Park Avenue.

but putting such frilly clothes on a boy was unusual. Ernest and Marcelline had identical dolls and matching tea sets. On a photograph of the children taken a month before Ernest's second birthday, Grace Hemingway wrote, "two summer girls."

Ernest's mother had gray eyes, light brown hair, and a contralto voice that was as soft and lush as velvet. She had trained for a career in opera, and she even sang once at Madison Square Garden, an arena in New York City. But the bright stage lights hurt her eyes, which had been weakened by scarlet fever in childhood, so she gave up performing and returned home. In 1896, she married Dr. Hemingway, who had grown up in the house across the street. Young Dr. Ed had cared for Grace's mother when she was dying of cancer.

Grace Hemingway may have settled for being a doctor's wife, but she dressed like an opera star in stylish gowns and costly hats with ostrich plumes. She viewed cleaning as the hired housekeeper's work and demanded breakfast in bed. Her tall, dark-haired husband often did the marketing, cooked meals, and canned fruits and vegetables. Once he interrupted a visit to a patient to phone home and ask to have his pie taken out of the oven.

As soon as he could, Ed Hemingway whisked Ernest away from doll carriages and taught him to love the outdoors. He took the boy fishing on his third birthday and, as Ernest grew older, showed him how to row a boat, start a fire, clean and cook a fish, make wild-onion sandwiches, and handle a gun.

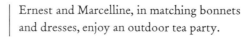

Ernest and Marcelline, in matching bonnets and dresses, enjoy an outdoor tea party.

Many of these lessons took place near Walloon Lake, in Michigan, where the Hemingways had a cottage called Windemere. There, sturdy little Ernest ran barefoot through the hemlock woods or along the beach. He got to know the local people, including some Ottawa Indians. Among them was Simon Green, a prosperous farmer who hunted partridge with Dr. Hemingway. Nick Boulton and Billy Tabeshaw, the two Indians Ernest knew best, sawed lumber. Nick was as brawny as Billy was squat. Sometimes the Hemingways invited Harold Sampson, a boy from Oak Park, to come to Windemere as Ernest's companion.

Everyone had chores to do in Michigan. Each day, Ernest fetched a pail of milk from the farm of a neighbor, Henry Bacon. Once, running home from Bacon's farm with a stick in his mouth, Ernest fell on his face, forcing the sharp wood into the tender flesh at the back of his throat. With calm, sure hands, Dr. Hemingway removed the stick and cauterized the wound with hot iron to stop it from bleeding and prevent infection. Years later, in his fiction, Hemingway recalled the softness of the pine needles that blanketed the trail to the farm and the fallen logs that rotted in the woods. But the pain and fear this injury caused were memories he kept to himself.

As a child and teenager, Hemingway spent summers with his family at Windemere Cottage.

Ed Hemingway stayed home for part of each summer to care for his patients and wrote letters to his family at Windemere. Shortly before Ernest's eighth birthday, he wrote to tell the boy that he had spied a gray cat in the backyard chicken coop. He had hurried to fetch a rifle, and as soon as the cat emerged, he fired. "Mr. Tom Cat turned a summersault in the air and will never steal eggs or baby chickens again," he reported.

Dr. Hemingway joined his wife and children in Michigan as often as he could. Wearing a straw hat and roomy old clothes, he fished on the lake in his rowboat, the *Marcelline of Windemere*. Medicine was far from

Grace and Clarence Edmonds Hemingway pose with their three oldest offspring. The children, from left to right, are Ursula, Ernest, and Marcelline.

his thoughts as he taught the children about the natural world. "Daddy could make any walk into a pleasure because he knew how to look at nature," said Marcelline. "He could make you see things you had never known were there."

At home in Oak Park, Ernest played at being a soldier or Pawnee Bill, the star of a traveling wild-west show. "When asked what he is afraid of," Grace Hemingway wrote, "he shouts out 'fraid of nothing' with great gusto." Five-year-old Ernest belonged to the Agassiz Club, a nature-study group founded by his father. The boys in this club, which was named for the nineteenth-century biologist Louis Agassiz, hiked through the woods and along the Des Plaines River, gathering plant specimens and learning to identify birds by their songs.

In April 1902, Ernest and Marcelline had welcomed a new sister, Ursula. Ernest wished for a brother when a fourth child was born, in November 1904, but the baby was another girl, Madelaine, who was called Sunny. Grandfather Hall died in May 1905, and the Hemingways sold his old-fashioned Victorian house. Grace used her inheritance to build a spacious home for her growing family on a corner lot at 600 North Kenilworth Avenue in Oak Park.

Grace planned the new house to be modern and showy, with three stories and eight bedrooms. A balcony hung over the music room, where she gave lessons. There was an office for Ed, so he, too, could work at home. Patients sitting in his waiting room gazed at the snakes, birds, and small mammals that the doctor had killed and preserved in jars and placed on display. The Hemingways also bought Longfield Farm, across the lake from Windemere, and Ed planned to grow fruit and hardwood trees on some of its forty acres.

In fall 1905, Ernest and Marcelline entered the first grade together. They were no longer Grace's twins—Ernest's brown hair had been cut short, and he wore boys' clothes—but they remained playmates. In winter, they skated for miles on the Des Plaines River. As they grew older, they read the books that filled the family's shelves. Ernest read classic adventure novels like *Ivanhoe* and *Robinson Crusoe,* and *True to the Old Flag,* a spirited children's book about the American Revolution. Later on, he loved the novels of Robert Louis Stevenson, especially *The Suicide Club,* a suspenseful story about a secret brotherhood whose members want to end their own lives.

The house at 600 North Kenilworth Avenue was roomy enough for a family of eight.

Ed and Grace Hemingway encouraged their children to read, but they banned any books that seemed coarse or common. They disapproved of writers like Jack London, who wrote brutal stories about life in the wilderness. When Ernest and Marcelline's seventh-grade class read *The Call of the Wild,* London's harsh, violent novel about an Alaskan sled dog, Grace went to the school and complained. "It's not the kind of book young people should be reading," she informed their teacher.

As devout members of the Third Congregational Church, Ernest's parents insisted that Sundays be set aside for prayer. Dr. Hemingway spanked any of his children who played on the Lord's Day, using the leather strop with which he sharpened his razor. Then, with his eyes flashing and his mouth drawn into a thin line, he made the child kneel and ask God's forgiveness.

At times, Ernest's father invented punishments to match his son's offenses. He did this in the summer of 1911, when Ernest and his friend Harold Sampson shot a porcupine while hunting in Michigan. Ed Hemingway scolded the twelve-year-olds for killing a harmless animal of the forest. It was true that he'd shot the thieving tomcat and killed small creatures for scientific display, but he never fired at an animal for no reason. To teach the boys a lesson, he ordered them to skin the porcupine, roast the meat over an open fire, and eat it. "We cooked the haunches for hours but they were still about as tender and tasty as a piece of shoe leather," Harold said.

As a teenager, Ernest bristled at his father's strictness. More than once, he sat in the doorway of the woodshed at Windemere and glared at Ed tending his tomato plants and sweating under the sun. Ernest would pick up his loaded shotgun, take careful aim at his father's head—and then lower the gun to the floor. Hemingway brought this to mind years later, when he was writing a story called "Fathers and Sons." His character, Nick Adams, remembers pointing a gun at his father and telling himself, "I can blow him to hell. I can kill him."

It was easier to feel powerful holding a gun in Michigan than trying to fit in as a freshman at Oak Park and River Forest High School. At fourteen, Ernest was five feet, four inches tall, nearly a head shorter than

Marcelline and too small for football. But he had big dreams and poured his private thoughts into his notebooks. "I desire to do pioneering or exploring work in the 3 last great frontiers Africa, southern central South America or the country around and north of Hudson Bay," he confided there. "I intend to specialize in the sciences in college and to join some expedition when I leave college. . . . I have no desire absolutely to be a millionaire or a rich man but I do intend to do something toward the scientific interests of the world."

He studied subjects that prepared him for college, including English literature and composition, Latin, science, and mathematics. He played the cello in the school orchestra, and he took dancing lessons with Marcelline after school. And at last, in the summer of 1914, when he turned fifteen, he grew, gaining an inch or more each month. He spent that summer raising vegetables with Harold Sampson at Longfield Farm, and by fall he was big and strong enough to play football. "You have grown to be such a fine big manly fellow," his father wrote when Ernest turned sixteen, "and [I] will trust your development will continue symmetrical and in harmony with our highest Christian ideals."

Ernest became a fan of boxing after seeing a prizefight in nearby Chicago in 1916. A friend of his father's took him to a gym where he could watch fighters train, and before long, he was sparring at home with his high school pals. Many of their fights took place in Grace Hemingway's music room, when Grace was out. "We girls watched from the balcony and teased the fighters by throwing paper wads and pillows down on top of them," said Marcelline. As an adult, Hemingway told

Ernest, who is about fourteen years old in this photograph, shows off a bird he has shot.

his friends that he had boxed with professional fighters in his youth and that a powerful blow to the head had damaged his vision. In truth, he did have a weak left eye, but he was born with it. The boxing story was as fanciful as his claim of stopping a runaway horse at age five.

Always ready to take a hike or a canoe trip, talk about the latest boxing match, or trade jokes, Ernest was popular with the boys. They had several nicknames for him: Hem, Oinbones, Hemingstein. The last one amused him most because it sounded like a Jewish name. Like many young people in narrow-minded Oak Park, Ernest grew up thinking it was all right to make fun of people of different faiths and backgrounds, and he never fully let go of this attitude. As an adult he occasionally called himself Hemingstein, or just Stein, and although he had Jewish friends, he sometimes mocked them behind their backs.

Teenager Ernest was shy with girls and took Marcelline to the junior-senior prom. "Ernie was a handsome boy," said one of his female classmates, "but he did not care how he looked. Unkempt is the only word to describe him."

By this time, there were six Hemingway children. A girl, named Carol, was born in 1911, and a boy, called Leicester (pronounced Lester), was born in 1915. Ernest nicknamed the baby Leicester De Pester. At last he had a brother, but the great difference in their ages meant that they would miss out on the closeness that comes from growing up together.

Now, at summer's start, Ernest traveled to Michigan with his friends. In June 1916, he and his pal Lew Clarahan took a steamboat across Lake Michigan and hiked inland to the town of Kalkaska. From there, Lew caught a train home, while Ernest trekked on alone to ready Windemere for the family's arrival. He opened shutters, uncovered chimneys, and raked up leaves and fallen branches that littered the ground.

That summer, Ernest slept in a tent pitched behind Windemere or at Longfield Farm, or he camped at Murphy's Point, half a mile away. He went often to the little community of Horton Bay to see his new friends Bill and Katy Smith, who spent summers with their aunt. Blond, slender Bill was twenty and in college. His green-eyed sister, Katy, whose untamable hair always fell into her face, was twenty-four. Bill and Katy nick-

A Hemingway family portrait. Leicester and Carol stand in front. The others, left to right, are Ed, Sunny, Grace, Marcelline, Ernest, and Ursula.

named Ernest "Wemedge." The three friends loved to laugh and got along well. They caught trout in the icy water of Horton Creek and relaxed afterward in the Smiths' cottage, talking about authors and books.

Bill and Ernest admired Rudyard Kipling, who wrote often about British-ruled India, where he had been born. "I thought he was the best short story writer that ever lived," Ernest said. He read and reread stories with ironic plot twists or macabre endings, such as "At the End of the Passage." In this story, isolation and hellish heat drive a British civil servant in India to madness and death. In another story that Ernest liked, "The Strange Ride of Morrowbie Jukes," a British engineer in India falls into a colony of social outcasts imprisoned by high walls of sand.

The young men also looked up to the popular English novelist Hugh Walpole, who preached a doctrine of strength and sufferance. "'Tisn't life that matters! 'Tis the courage you bring to it," Walpole wrote in his novel

Fortitude. The hero of this story, a boy named Peter Westcott, passes repeated tests of courage. He is beaten by his abusive father, attends a wretched boarding school, and sees his mother die. At the novel's end, Peter prays, "Make of me a man—to be afraid of nothing."

Ernest began writing short stories of his own. At home in Oak Park, he often retreated to the third floor, away from the family's noise, to concentrate at his typewriter. Some of his stories appeared in the high school literary magazine, the *Tabula*. Mistaken revenge leads to tragedy in one story, "The Judgment of Manitou." (*Manitou* is the Ottawa word for God.) When a trapper, a Cree Indian named Pierre, believes that his partner, Dick Haywood, has stolen his wallet, he sets a trap for the unwary man. Then, too late, Pierre discovers the real thief: a red squirrel. He runs through the frigid winter woods to save his partner but arrives to see animals scavenging on Haywood's body. Pierre takes his own life for what he has done, to "save My-in-gau, the wolf, the trouble."

"Sepi Jingan" is a tale like those by Jack London, an adventure story about an Indian with the same name as Ernest's friend in Michigan, Billy Tabeshaw, whose life is saved by his loyal dog. After his cousin is murdered, Billy pursues the killer through the wild. The murderer surprises Billy, however, and is about to kill him when the dog, Sepi Jingan, leaps, "like a shaggy thunderbolt," and breaks the man's neck with his "wolf jaws."

Sometimes Ernest tried to sound like another writer he admired, Ring Lardner. Lardner wrote a popular sports column for the *Chicago Tribune* and humorous short stories in which he captured the speech of ordinary Americans. His story "Gullible's Travels," about a middle-class couple who try to mingle with high society, begins: "I promised the Wife that if anybody ast me what kind of a time did I have at Palm Beach I'd say I had a swell time. And if they ast me who did we meet I'd tell 'em everybody that was worth meetin'."

Calling himself Ring Lardner Junior, Ernest reported on athletic events for the school newspaper, the *Trapeze*. In a story about a swimming meet between the Oak Park and Evanston, Illinois, high schools, he wrote, "Evanston wasn't no meat for us in that swimming meet. But if we would have got 20 more points we would have beat them." At other times he

Ring Lardner writes a story in his office at the *Chicago Tribune.* Hemingway mimicked Lardner's folksy style in his high school reporting.

used his real name and a more standard writing style to report news from the school and community.

Ernest's teachers praised his writing and read his compositions aloud to their classes. One of his favorite English teachers, Miss Margaret Dixon, had strong opinions and an equally keen temper. She praised her students' work when it met her high expectations and criticized it to pieces when it fell short. Seeing that Ernest showed unusual ability, she prodded him to use his imagination and be original.

Another favorite English teacher, Miss Fannie Biggs, also encouraged Ernest. Miss Biggs was a tiny woman who inspired her students to be creative. Once, she came to Ernest's defense when his writing got him into trouble. This happened when five boys, including Ernest, made a secret newspaper called the *Jazz Journal.* They filled it with dirty jokes and passed it around to their friends.

The principal, Mr. McDaniel, got hold of the journal and called its authors into his office. Ernest hated "Gum Shoe Mac" McDaniel, who acted

Teacher Fannie Biggs visits the Hemingways in 1916. In this picture, Grace stands to the left, holding Carol by the arm; Ursula is behind her. Sunny stands next to her mother, and Marcelline is behind Sunny. Miss Biggs looks at Ernest, who holds Leicester's hands. The identity of the fellow peeking over Miss Biggs's shoulder has been lost to history.

like a detective, keeping a suspicious eye on everyone, students and teachers alike. Some of the teachers believed that he climbed into the school's attic and spied through the ventilation ducts into their classrooms.

The *Jazz Journal* lay on the principal's desk. He could expel the boys for writing it, McDaniel said, but they would escape punishment this time. Why? Because a teacher had come forward to say that she had lectured them about their wrongdoing, and that they had promised to make no more journals. The teacher was Miss Biggs, who had lied on their behalf.

As graduation neared, Ernest thought about his future. His parents wanted him to go to college like Marcelline, who planned to study music at Oberlin College in Ohio. They hoped that he might become a doctor, like his father. Three years earlier, Ernest had considered studying science in college. But in 1917, he craved adventure, and he balked at the idea of four more years of school.

One place to find excitement was Europe. Across the Atlantic, the desire of small European cultural groups for independence, the emergence of Germany as a world power, and a buildup of arms had exploded in bloodshed in 1914. The resulting war pitted the Allies—including Great Britain, France, tsarist Russia, and Italy—against the Central Powers—Germany, Austria-Hungary, Turkey, and Bulgaria. The United States had tried to stay out of the conflict, but when Germany disrupted shipping in the North Atlantic and began sinking American ships, it was time to take action. On April 6, 1917, the United States declared war on Germany and entered the First World War.

At train stations decked with banners and flags, Ernest saw youths not much older than himself heading for army training camps. He read *The Dark Forest,* Hugh Walpole's tear-jerking novel of World War I. In this book, a young Englishman serves as a volunteer with the Russian Red Cross, carrying wounded soldiers away from the battlefront. The hero falls in love with a beautiful nurse and, tragically, is killed by an Austrian bomb.

Ernest joked about the war in the speech he gave at his high school graduation. As class prophet, he looked into the future to predict where life would lead the senior class. He foresaw that some students would become army officers or Red Cross nurses. He said that one boy would save Oak Park by shooting hot air at German zeppelins. Another would grow wealthy selling gunpowder to the government. He also spotted a future lion tamer and a woman submarine diver among his classmates. Marcelline, he said, would become a "noted lady veterinarian" renowned for driving too fast and running over elderly pedestrians.

At home he talked about joining the army, but his parents would hear no talk of soldiering. At seventeen, he was much too young to see war, they said. Besides, the army would never take a young man with a weak left eye. He was old enough to work, though, and he liked writing. Why not work for a newspaper? His uncle Tyler Hemingway, who ran a lumber business in Kansas City, Missouri, had friends at the local paper, the *Star*. He asked about a job for his nephew and was told that Ernest could join the staff in October, replacing a reporter who was going to war.

After one last summer in Michigan, Ernest boarded a train for Kansas City. He never wrote about how it felt to leave his family, except possibly in his 1940 novel *For Whom the Bell Tolls*. The hero of this book, Robert Jordan, has a father much like Dr. Hemingway. At one point, Robert remembers the day he left for college, and how his father kissed him and uttered a prayer:

> His father had been a very religious man, and he had said it simply and sincerely. But his moustache had been moist and his eyes were damp with emotion and Robert Jordan had been so embarrassed by all of it, the damp religious sound of the prayer, and by his father kissing him good-by, that he had felt suddenly so much older than his father and sorry for him that he could hardly bear it.

THREE

Into the Furnace of Suffering

Ernest's uncle met him in the lobby of Union Station, Kansas City's busy rail terminal. This room was so large and lavish that people called it the Grand Hall. Its walls of mustard-colored stone rose ninety-five feet into the air to join a colorful carved ceiling. The sun shone through three arched windows that were taller and wider than any Ernest had ever seen.

Union Station was modern and new, like so much in Kansas City: the skyline of tall office buildings; the Trafficway Viaduct that carried cars, electric trains, and pedestrians high overhead; the system of boulevards that moved vehicles through the bustling city. Ernest took in the sights as his uncle drove him to quiet Warwick Boulevard, to a brick house with a perfect lawn where he lived with his wife, Arabella.

The next day, Tyler Hemingway escorted his nephew downtown to another new building, this one massively wide and three stories high. It housed the offices and presses of the *Kansas City Star*. Ernest and his uncle walked through the arched doorway, rode an elevator to the second story, and entered a noisy room that held endless rows of desks. Typewriters clacked and telephones rang nonstop. Every few minutes, a reporter called for the copyboy to pick up a finished story.

Union Station in Kansas City was bright, busy, and modern.

George Longan, the busy city editor, offered Ernest a job at fifteen dollars a week. He then turned the strong, healthy youth over to his assistant, Pete Wellington, who would be Ernest's boss. Wellington was a small man who looked as though he never left his desk to step out in the sun. He rarely smiled, but he took a kindly interest in the reporters who worked for him. "He had the wonderful habit of putting his arm around you and then talking to you as though he was a friend instead of a boss," said Russel Crouse, who wrote about sports for the *Star* in 1917.

Wellington expected his reporters to write stories that were accurate, stirring, and fresh. He held firm ideas about newspaper writing that could be summed up this way: "Use short sentences. Use short first paragraphs. Use vigorous English. Be positive, not negative." Hemingway never forgot these lessons and applied them to everything he wrote, throughout his life. "Those were the best rules I ever learned for the business of writing," he said much later, after he was famous. "No man with any talent, who feels and writes truly about the thing he is trying to say, can fail to write well if he abides by them."

Ernest Hemingway, cub reporter, rarely sat still. He befriended the cops at the No. 4 Police Station and rode along in their squad cars, looking for news. He wandered through Union Station, eyes and ears open, observing the people coming and going. He interviewed celebrities as they stepped off trains and got to know some "shady characters."

He spent so much time questioning accident and assault victims at

KANSAS CITY, MO — Home of "The Kansas City Star"

In 1917, the Kansas City Star Building looked much as it did on this 1924 postcard. The rooftop radio towers were new when this photograph was taken. Radio entertainment first entered people's homes in the 1920s.

General Hospital that its antiseptic smell lingered in his nostrils. More than once, Pete Wellington called the hospital looking for Ernest, only to learn that he was off in an ambulance, speeding to the site of a crash or shooting. "He always wanted to be on the scene himself," Wellington said.

Like all the young reporters, Ernest looked up to Lionel Moise, a heavy-drinking newspaperman with a reputation for brawling. Here was someone who knew how to live and write! Moise was a tall, husky man whose thick fingers moved swiftly over his typewriter keys. He could juggle five stories at once and have them all polished by press time, with "something alive about each one," Hemingway said. This seasoned reporter filled his stories with action and dialogue, avoiding descriptions that slowed the pace. "The only way to improve your writing is to write," he told Ernest—when he was in a talking mood.

In late October, Ernest moved into an apartment with Carl Edgar, who knew Bill Smith, Ernest's friend from Horton Bay. They each paid $2.50 a week for a big room with easy chairs and a sleeping porch with two beds. Carl worked for a fuel-oil company and was hopelessly in love with Bill's sister, Katy. Many nights, easygoing "Odgar" stayed up late, listening to Ernest jabber about "the romance of newspaper work." On other nights, Ernest hung around the press room of the Hotel Muehlebach, where reporters often gathered. If he felt tired, he slept in the adjacent bathroom, using towels as a mattress and the tub as a bed.

Ernest was living by his own rules and not his parents'. Soon after Christmas, Grace Hemingway learned from Tyler and Arabella that he had stopped going to church. Immediately, she fired off an angry letter to her son, blaming Bill Smith and Carl Edgar for leading him astray. Ernest replied with excuses, claiming that he worked on Saturday nights and woke too late for church on Sundays. Besides, he added, people dressed too stylishly at his aunt and uncle's church, and he felt out of place there.

Then he expressed his real feelings. "Now mother I got awfully angry when I read what you wrote about Carl and Bill," he admitted. "Please don't unjustly criticize my friends again." Grace's rigid way of thinking—her unwillingness to tolerate other viewpoints—hurt, frustrated, and angered her older son. Over time, Ernest's feelings hardened into a strong dislike of his mother.

Ernest thought more about going to war, especially after meeting Ted Brumback, another rookie reporter for the *Star*. Ted had spent four months in Europe, driving an ambulance for the French army even though he was blind in one eye. He talked to Ernest about the thrill of being on the front lines and how he couldn't wait to return.

If someone with one seeing eye could drive an ambulance, then so could Ernest, with his less-than-perfect vision. In early spring, he and Ted signed up to be drivers for the American Red Cross, the organization that administered first aid at battle sites and carried wounded soldiers to hospitals. The Red Cross was recruiting men between the ages of eighteen and twenty to serve for six months with ambulance units in Italy.

On the last day of April, Ernest and Ted collected their paychecks and said good-bye to the staff of the *Star*. There was time for one last fishing trip before embarking for France—or so Ernest hoped. He headed for Horton Bay with Carl Edgar and Charlie Hopkins, another friend from Kansas City. Yet no sooner did he drop his hook in the water than a telegram came ordering him to be in New York City by May 8.

Ernest's parents were less than pleased, but at eighteen he was old enough to join the army without their permission. Ambulance work was safer than trench warfare, so they dropped their objections to his service overseas.

In New York, Ernest and Ted joined about seventy other men from all over the country. Some had volunteered for ambulance duty because they were too young to join the army, and others had been rejected by the military for disabilities like poor eyesight. There were also a few who longed for the adventure of war without all the dangers of battle. Ernest passed

The American Red Cross used posters like this one to recruit men as ambulance drivers. Rules changed as the war progressed. This poster, seeking volunteers at least thirty-one years old, was probably created in 1917. The men who responded served in France.

the physical exam but ignored the doctor's advice to get glasses. He purchased his uniform, with small red crosses on its shirt collar and cap, and expensive leather boots. He was to be stationed in Italy and held the honorary rank of second lieutenant in the Italian army.

On May 21, 1918, the volunteers set sail on the *Chicago,* an aging French ocean liner. In a letter, Ernest told his parents to "think of what the rottenest ship in the world is and you know what I am on." If he craved adventure, he seemed to have found it. For two days, the *Chicago* pitched wildly in stormy seas, battered by heavy winds and rain. The constant rolling made most of the men seasick, but Ernest bore it better than the rest, bragging that he "heaved but four times." The sea at last grew calm, but then the crew blackened the *Chicago*'s portholes to prevent the tired old ship from being spotted at night. The captain feared that U-boats—the dreaded German submarines—might be in the area.

Fortunately or not, depending on whether a young man hoped for safety or danger, the ship avoided any U-boats and docked at Bordeaux, in southwestern France. Immediately Ernest and Ted Brumback hopped on a Paris-bound train. Ernest was alive to every sight, sound, and motion, "as if he'd been sent on special assignment to cover the biggest story of the year," Brumback said.

Paris, when they arrived, was a city under siege, where shells fired by German long-range guns ripped through the air and exploded in the streets. Instead of seeking shelter, though, Ernest and Ted hired a taxi to take them to see the action. With each thundering boom, they raced through the streets only to hear the next blast farther away. When they at last saw a bursting shell strike La Madeleine, a historic church, they decided that they had witnessed enough destruction for one day.

In less than a week, the Red Cross volunteers boarded a train bound for northern Italy, where Italian forces were battling the Austrians to gain control of four border territories. Ernest and the others reached Milan in time to see a munitions factory explode—and to go to work. The volunteers put out any lingering fires; then they collected the bodies of dead factory workers. "I must admit, frankly, the shock it was to find out that those dead were women rather than men," Ernest wrote. The volunteers

Servicemen stare at what remains of a five-story U.S. supply depot that was destroyed in a German air raid on Paris. Wreckage like this was a common sight in the French capital when Hemingway and Brumback arrived.

also had the grim task of picking body parts from a barbed-wire fence.

The Red Cross assigned Ernest and Ted to Section Four, in the town of Schio, nestled in the low hills at the edge of the Dolomites. In peacetime, the people of this mountain region manufactured wool cloth. But with the coming of war, Schio's woolen factory served as the Red Cross barracks. The old building still smelled of sheep, and the Americans jokingly called it the Schio Country Club. At least the food was good: The men ate rich stews made with local game and steaming plates of pasta, and they washed it all down with robust red wine.

Ernest took turns with the others driving a big gray ambulance into the mountains. He picked up as many wounded men as his ambulance could carry, and then he cautiously maneuvered it down narrow, twisting roads to the Red Cross distribution center. There, doctors and nurses gave the men emergency care and arranged their transport to hospitals. Often the guns were quiet, and Ernest had time for sightseeing—more than enough time, he thought. "There's nothing here but scenery and too damn much of that," he complained to Ted Brumback. "I'm going to get out of this ambulance section and find out where the war is."

In mid-June, hard, uninterrupted fighting broke out along the Piave River, to the east. Austrian forces advanced across the river, and Italian and British units battled to drive them back. Shooting, shelling, and hand-to-hand combat went on for days. The warring grew so fierce that the Italian Supreme Command called the Piave region a "furnace of suffering."

So, of course, when the section chief asked for men to staff new canteens in the towns dotting the Piave River, Second Lieutenant Ernest Hemingway raised his hand. Throughout the war zone, the Red Cross operated roadside canteens, where off-duty soldiers could rest and write letters, enjoy hot coffee or soup, or pick up candy and cigarettes.

The Red Cross transported Ernest to the village of Fossalta, a mile and

American Red Cross ambulance volunteers stand with soldiers near the Piave River in 1917 or 1918.

A Red Cross volunteer gives chocolate to soldiers in the trenches along the Piave River.

a half from the front lines, where the stone buildings had been cracked and broken by enemy shelling. Ernest spent much of his time unpacking supplies. As the only American in town, he lived by himself in a small house. He had a talent for learning languages and practiced speaking Italian over dinner at the Italian officers' mess hall. He also made friends with a young priest from Florence, Don Giuseppe Bianchi. Twice a day, he bicycled to the battle lines, bringing postcards, chocolate, and cigarettes to the soldiers. "The Italians in the trenches got to know his smiling face," Ted Brumback said. Hemingway always carried a gas mask, helmet, and gun, in case he came under fire.

On the hot night of July 8, Ernest felt lonely, as he often did in Fossalta, and pedaled to the riverbank to be near the soldiers. He stood at a listening post, a spot near the enemy line where the Italian soldiers strained their ears to detect the sounds of troop movement, and looked out over the water. By this time, the Italians had recaptured their positions along the Piave, but the conflict continued. From muddy trenches that stretched for miles along the river's west bank, Italian infantrymen traded fire with the Austrians on the other side. Every so often, an exploding shell cast shimmering light on the water.

Around midnight, the shooting intensified. Ernest put on his helmet, ducked down, and hurried toward the trenches. Huddled in their earthen shelter, he and the soldiers heard a strange sound—*"chuh—chuh—chuh—chuh"*—that grew into a roar. Their surroundings disappeared in a great flash of light, first white and then red. It came from an exploding Austrian shell that forced the air out of Ernest's lungs. He would relive the sensations of this night when writing *A Farewell to Arms*. "I tried to breathe, but my breath would not come," he remembered. Within moments, he could see again: "The ground was torn up and in front of my head there was a splintered beam of wood." Beside him lay a man who neither moved nor made sound, but beyond the dead soldier another man moaned.

Ernest stood up. His feet felt as though he had plunged them into rubber boots filled with hot water, but he seemed to have escaped serious injury. He carefully lifted the wounded soldier, and with the man's weight over his shoulder, he headed for the command post. He had three hundred feet to cross when a machine-gun bullet tore into his right knee, feeling "like a sharp smack on the leg with an icy snow ball." He fell in pain, but he got back on his feet. Still carrying his load, he covered the remaining ground—he never knew how.

So much of the soldier's blood had soaked into Ernest's clothes that his "coat and pants looked like someone had made currant jelly in them," he said. The army medic thought he had been shot in the chest, but his wounds were limited to his legs and feet. Not only had he been shot, but shrapnel from the exploding artillery shell had torn up his flesh. The wetness he'd felt was his own blood.

Ernest Hemingway waited two hours among the other casualties to be evacuated by ambulance. Surrounded by so many suffering men, he felt that dying was the natural thing to do, and he remembered the pistol he had been issued when he joined the Red Cross. "How much better to die in all the happy period of undisillusioned youth, to go out in a blaze of light," he thought. He went on living, though, and when he at last reached a field hospital, doctors removed twenty-eight metal fragments from his legs. Many more remained.

Hemingway's next destination was the American Red Cross Hospital in Milan. On the morning of July 15, orderlies lifted him onto a railroad car. With his wounds "hurting like 227 little devils driving nails into the raw," he lay for hours in the heat, waiting for the train to move and watching flies land on his bandages. At last the train lurched forward, and two days later, it reached Milan. Doctors there x-rayed Ernest's legs and saw a machine-gun bullet in his right foot and a second one behind his right kneecap. They removed these in the operating room. "The Italian surgeon did a peach of an operation on my right knee joint and my right foot," Ernest reported to his family at home.

"This is a peach of a hospital here," Ernest informed his family, and "Milan is a peach of a town." They sent him clippings from the Oak Park and Chicago newspapers, which had carried the story of his wounding. "It's the next best thing to getting killed and reading your own obituary," he replied. Marcelline wrote to say that she had gone to the movies and spotted him in a newsreel. The next day, all the Hemingways went to see him on the big screen. Soon there was more good news: Ernest had been

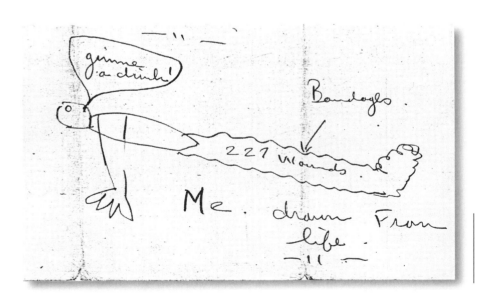

Ernest drew this picture of his wounded self in a letter to his family dated July 21, 1918.

nominated for the silver medal of valor, an Italian award for bravery, and he would be promoted to first lieutenant.

Feeling like the man of the hour, Ernest made friends with the nurses. With only four patients to care for, the eighteen Red Cross nurses had time to relax. Ernest got to know middle-aged Elsie Macdonald from Scotland, who cared for him *"like a good mother,"* she said. Ernest was her "dear broken doll." He teasingly called her the Spanish Mackerel and convinced her to look the other way if a hospital worker smuggled in cognac for him.

And then there was the pretty night nurse, Agnes von Kurowsky, who was twenty-six years old and from Washington, D.C. Agnes called Ernest Kid, so he nicknamed her Mrs. Kid and said he would marry her one day. Like the hero of *The Dark Forest,* he had fallen in love with a nurse.

Agnes grew to care for the handsome, ruddy young hero and sat with him often, holding hands and exchanging kisses. The Red Cross had a rule against nurses dating their patients, so when Ernest was strong enough to walk with crutches or a cane, he and Agnes went out in the company of others. One happy day, they went to watch horseraces with Elsie Macdonald and two recovering pilots.

In late September, Ernest felt well enough for a trip to Lake Maggiore, on the Swiss border, with Johnny Miller, an ambulance driver from Minnesota. He returned to Milan to hear crushing news: Agnes was about to leave. A hospital in Florence had been hit by an outbreak of influenza and needed nurses desperately. In 1918 a merciless form of influenza swept through the world and

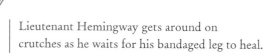
Lieutenant Hemingway gets around on crutches as he waits for his bandaged leg to heal.

Hemingway had his picture taken with men and nurses of the Red Cross at the hospital in Milan. Agnes von Kurowsky stands to his left.

claimed tens of millions of lives. As a result, half the U.S. servicemen who died in Europe succumbed to infectious disease, which the American Medical Association called "the greatest enemy of all."

For a time, daily letters traveled between Florence and Milan. "The Light of My Existence, My Dearest and Best, Most Ernest of Ernies, More Precious Than Gold, and My Hero," Agnes wrote.

Ernest went back to the front in late October, although he was still too weak to drive an ambulance. The appearance of jaundice—yellow skin that may signal a liver ailment—brought him again to the hospital. This time, as he waited to recover, he traded war stories with a twenty-three-year-old British officer, Eric Edward Dorman-Smith, who seemed like a character in an adventure tale. Dorman-Smith's friends called him Chink because, with his narrow face and pointed ears, he resembled his regiment's mascot, the chinkara, an Asian gazelle. He had been fighting the enemy in Belgium and Italy since 1914, and he had been wounded three times. When he met Ernest, he was being treated for an intestinal illness. Agnes visited briefly and then rushed off to Treviso, near the city of Padua, where American soldiers were dying of influenza.

One day in December, Agnes saw a familiar figure coming through a Treviso hospital ward. A tall young man in a spotless uniform with a shiny medal pinned to his chest was marching around, leaning on a cane. He boasted of his battle scars to anyone who would listen, talking in too loud a voice. It was Ernest, and he had come to see her. Agnes noticed something else that Ernest failed to see: The soldiers in the hospital beds were laughing at him behind his back.

Agnes was a grown woman doing necessary work, and there was Ernest acting like a boy. She told her young lover to go home. The warring nations had signed an armistice on November 11, 1918. The Allies had won, and the world was at peace. It was time for Ernest to end his Italian escapade, return to the United States, and get on with his life. The Red Cross still needed her in Italy, but in a year or two they might possibly be married.

On January 4, 1919, Ernest sailed from the port of Genoa aboard the *Giuseppe Verdi,* an Italian steamship bound for New York. He went home changed, having seen the destruction and suffering caused by war. He had learned how it felt to have his courage tested; he had even fallen in love. He carried home a wealth of experience to feed his writing. "I've only got about 50 more years to live," he wrote to Bill Smith, "and I don't want to waste any of them."

FOUR

A Stranger at Home

The *Giuseppe Verdi* docked in New York City on January 21, 1919, and a splendid hero limped down the gangplank. Wearing polished leather boots and the flowing black cape of an Italian army officer, Ernest Hemingway quickly won the admiration of a reporter for the *New York Sun*. This fearless soldier had withstood more pain than "any other man, in or out of uniform, who defied the shrapnel of the Central Powers," the journalist marveled.

A train carried Ernest to Chicago, where he was met by his father and Marcelline. Then, before he knew it, the wounded officer was home. He endured his family's hugs and read the letters from Agnes that had reached Oak Park before he did. "How I wish I knew how you are at this moment," she wrote.

Days passed, and Ernest settled into a lazy routine. He lay in bed until noon, covered with a shawl from Italy. After joining his family for lunch, he walked the streets of Oak Park, wearing his uniform and cape and leaning on a cane. Although he was a hero in the eyes of the town, he slept at night with a light on. The war had shown him unspeakable sights that would forever haunt him: bodies left unburied on Italian mountain-

Ernest's uniform, cape, and cane set him apart from the other residents of Oak Park.

sides in the aftermath of battle, blackening in the sun; maggots eating away the mouths of corpses; a general whose head had been blown open by a bullet and whose blood reddened the snow.

The local newspaper printed a story about this hometown celebrity, and Italian Americans from Chicago came to honor him with spaghetti and wine. The noisy party was incomplete until they had hung the Italian flag from the balcony in Grace Hemingway's music room and sung arias from Italian operas. Ernest's father tried to be a good sport, but he frowned on drinking alcohol. When the Italians showed up a second time, he marched angrily to bed.

On March 14, Ernest spoke during an assembly at his old high school. He still wore his officer's uniform, although he had been home from

GATHERING IN HONOR OF
LIEUT. ERNEST HEMINGWAY
FEB. 16, 1919

When Italian Americans gathered in Grace Hemingway's music room
to honor Ernest, a professional photographer recorded the event.
Ernest sits toward the center of the middle row, in front of his parents.

Europe for nearly two months. The students sat enthralled as he described being wounded and held up the "punctured trousers" in which he had survived the night on the Piave. He showed off his other souvenirs as well: an Austrian revolver, a gas mask, and his medals, including one he claimed had been bestowed by the king of Italy himself.

The dashing clothes, heroic tales, and long mornings in bed were outward signs of changes within. Traveling to Europe and tasting war had broadened Ernest's outlook. He had been set apart from his family and most ordinary Americans, and knew he never would be happy in Oak Park again.

Hemingway explored this state of mind in the short story "Soldier's Home," about a Marine named Harold Krebs who returns to Oklahoma after fighting in World War I. Krebs, like Ernest, feels distanced from the people around him. He likes watching girls walk along the street, "But the world they were in was not the world he was in." Krebs's mother sounds like pious Grace Hemingway when she tells him, "God has some work for every one to do. . . . There can be no idle hands in His Kingdom." Krebs replies starkly, "I'm not in His Kingdom." She asks, "Don't you love your mother, dear boy?" and he answers, "No."

Ernest felt even more adrift in late March, when Agnes told him in a letter that she had fallen in love with a handsome Italian lieutenant. Heartbroken and angry, he wrote to Elsie Macdonald that he hoped Agnes would fall on her face and knock out her front teeth! However, he found it impossible to stay angry, and by June, referring to his romance with Agnes, he was able to say, "That's all shut behind me."

As the days grew warmer, he put away his uniform and cape, and he began to write stories like "The Passing of Pickles McCarty," which dealt with an American boxer who fought the Austrians in Italy. He sent his stories to the *Saturday Evening Post* and other popular magazines; the editors always sent them back, but with each one, he learned to be a better writer.

Ernest went to Horton Bay to spend the summer with Bill Smith, camping, fishing, and writing. His heart was healing, and he dated a girl named Marjorie Bump, who worked nearby as a waitress. It was a summer of wading into icy streams with a baited hook, savoring breakfasts of fresh-caught trout fried with bacon, and strolling beside the bay, dazzled by the reflection of the setting sun.

Ernest took his final camping trip of the year in August, with an old friend from high school, Jack Pentecost, and another young man named Al Walker. The three went far to the north, to the town of Seney, Michigan, close to Lake Superior and Canada. As their train approached Seney, Ernest heard the brakeman tell the engineer to wait longer than usual before leaving the station. "There's a cripple and he needs time to get his stuff down," the brakeman said. Ernest knew the brakeman was talking

Leicester's toy car is the ambulance when Ernest and a friend play a game of rescue.

about him, and it shocked him to think that people saw him in this way. He vowed never again to be weak in body or mind.

Ernest stayed in Michigan at summer's end to write. He rented a room in the town of Petoskey and worked afternoons shoveling gravel to cover his expenses. In December he spoke about his wartime exploits to the Petoskey Ladies' Aid Society. Afterward, a well-dressed member of the audience came up to him and introduced herself. She was Harriet Connable, the wife of Ralph Connable, who headed the Canadian branch of the F. W. Woolworth chain of stores. Mr. and Mrs. Connable and their grown daughter planned to spend the winter in Florida, but they needed someone to stay in Toronto with Ralph Junior, a teenager who had some physical disabilities. The job was Ernest's if he wanted it, Mrs. Connable said, and Ernest told her that he did.

Being young Ralph's companion turned out to be easy. The Connables lived in a mansion with a library, a billiard room, a skating rink, and servants. Ralph Junior studied with a tutor each morning and worked for his father's company in the afternoon. Ernest's only task was to accompany the boy if he went to an evening boxing match or hockey game. For this he received fifty dollars a month, plus expenses.

Ernest had lots of free time for writing, and he spent some of it reporting for the *Toronto Star*. He wrote articles on light topics, like the "Circulating Pictures" movement. This was his name for the trend among city matrons to rent paintings rather than buy them from artists. He wrote, too, about the harrowing experience of being shaved by a beginner at the local barbers' school.

When summer returned, he went back to Michigan—and back to his parents' nagging. He turned twenty-one in July, and they wanted to know why he wasn't going to college or buckling down to work. His father hated the "vitriolistic words" that seasoned his speech. And his mother complained that he would still rather fish than wash dishes or bury the trash, yet he ate lustily at the family table.

To prove that he could feed himself, as well as to upset his mother, Ernest bragged that he would eat a snipe. He shot one of the little wading birds, cleaned it, tore its flesh with his teeth, and swallowed it raw. "Downy snipe feathers littered the sand below the tall tamaracks," Leicester recalled. "Mother was terribly distressed. It was not just that the snack had been so 'uncivilized.' It seemed a brutal needling of her complaints that Ernest was decreasing the family larder while continuing to be a bum."

That summer, Ted Brumback came to stay at Windemere too. One night, Ursula and Sunny invited Ernest and Ted to come on a late-night adventure. Just after midnight, the four sneaked out of the house. They met up with some teenagers from the neighboring Loomis cottage and boated across the lake to a spot called Ryan's Point. There, they lit a bonfire and spent a couple of hours picnicking, swimming, and having fun. It was three A.M. when they put out the fire and rowed over the dark water toward home. As they neared the shore, they saw Grace Hemingway and Mrs. Loomis waiting. The empty beds had been discovered, and the two mothers were furious.

The next day, Grace ordered Ernest and Ted to leave Windemere at once. She blamed them for the night's antics, because they should have known better at their age, and she declared them a bad influence on the girls. She related to her husband what happened next: "Ernest called me every name he could think of, and said everything vile about me."

Instead of losing her temper, Grace handed Ernest a cold, careful, cruel letter that compared a mother's love to money in a bank, which could be counted and spent. A mother draws from this limited amount of love as she cares for her son through childhood, Grace explained. It was up to the son, as he grew older, to make deposits in the account through good behavior and tokens of affection, to prevent her love from running out. "Unless you, my son, Ernest, come to yourself, cease your lazy loafing, and pleasure seeking," she continued, "unless, in other words, you come into your manhood—there is nothing before you but bankruptcy: *You have over drawn.*"

She sent a copy of this letter to Ed Hemingway, who approved of the way she had handled their wrong-headed son. It was high time for Ernest to "get busy and make his own way, and suffering alone will be the means of softening his Iron Heart of selfishness," he wrote to his wife.

Ernest had provoked his mother's anger, but her sharp words cut straight to his heart. He made no reply; he just deposited a little more hatred in his own account and took off for a fishing trip with Ted, Jack Pentecost, and some other chums. He talked about shipping to the Far East, but instead he went to Chicago, where he stayed with Bill and Katy's older brother, Yeremya Kenley "Y. K." Smith, and looked for a job.

Smoky, noisy, and bustling with life, Chicago in 1920 stood for commerce and growth. Thirty-nine railroad lines converged on the Windy City to carry the bounty of midwestern farms to markets throughout the nation. Fifty thousand people came to live there every year, many from as far away as Italy, Greece, Poland, and Hungary. Immigrants joined the great number of men and women who traveled daily to and from jobs in the city center. A two-level bridge spanning the Chicago River had opened to the public on May 14, and the world's largest rail terminal was under construction. Plans called for a mammoth new post office, new playgrounds, and more public beaches along Lake Michigan.

A lively bunch of friends dropped in at the place Y. K. shared with his wife, Doodles. Through the couple, Ernest had a happy reunion with Bill Horne, a fellow ambulance driver in Italy who was working for a company called Standard Parts. He also met Y. K.'s friend Sherwood Anderson, a writer who was newly famous. The linked stories in Anderson's book *Winesburg, Ohio* examined the failures and isolation of people living in one small American town at the end of the nineteenth century. With simple words, Anderson created penetrating portraits that were beautiful in their spareness. Yet his straightforward sentences sounded like prose that was meant to be read aloud to children:

Pistols are aimed in fun as this group of friends clowns in summer 1920. From left to right are Carl Edgar, Katy Smith, Marcelline, Bill Horne, Ernest, and Bill Smith.

The writer, an old man with a white mustache, had some difficulty in getting into bed. The windows of the house in which he lived were high and he wanted to look at the trees when he awoke in the morning. A carpenter came to fix the bed so that it would be on a level with the window.

Anderson liked to tell new friends that he had been a businessman until the day in 1912 when he had left his desk in the middle of dictating a letter, walked out of his office, and never gone back. He was twice Hemingway's age, but a youthful energy lit up his dark eyes when he talked about things that excited him, like horseracing or writing. He saw that Hemingway was "a young fellow of extraordinary talent," and "an American writer instinctively in touch with everything worth-while going on here." He took the younger man under his wing, and Ernest often visited Anderson and his wife, Tennessee, at their home outside the city.

In October, Katy Smith's old friend Hadley Richardson visited from St. Louis. Hadley had spent a quiet, sheltered life studying piano and had nursed her mother through a long, fatal illness. She had come to Chicago hoping the change of scenery would brighten her spirits. Hadley liked all the Smiths' friends, especially the big, handsome charmer they called Wemedge. He had "a pair of very red cheeks and very brown eyes," she observed, and his zest won him the admiration of every person in the room. He was also accomplished: He could box, fish, and write.

Sherwood Anderson gave up a business career and chose a writer's life.

Ernest felt a strong attraction to this tall young woman with rust-colored hair that he likened to love at first sight. "I knew she was the girl I was going to marry," he later told his brother, Leicester. Like Agnes, Hadley was seven years older than Ernest. He saw her every day while she was in Chicago, and he wrote to her when she went home to St. Louis. Still looking for a steady job, he moved into a rented room with Bill

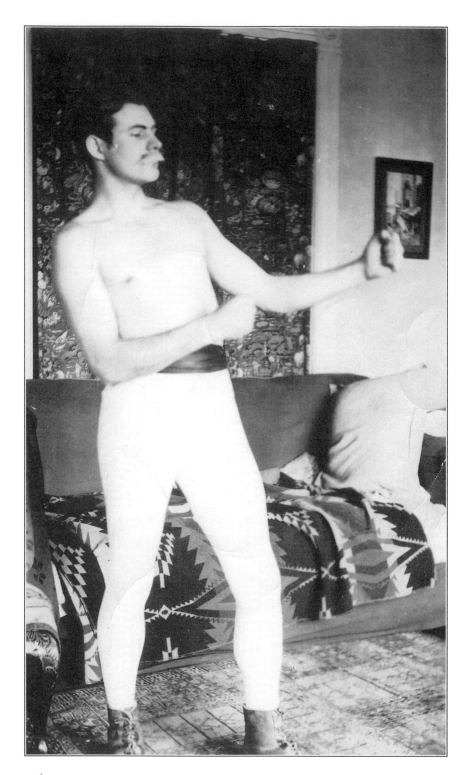

While staying with Y. K. Smith in Chicago, Ernest dons a
false mustache and pretends to be John L. Sullivan, a boxing
champion of the 1880s and 1890s.

Horne. Now and then he wrote articles for the *Toronto Star* and advertisements for tires. From these he earned enough money to eat at the Kitsos Lunchroom, where a plate of steak and potatoes cost sixty cents.

At last, in December, a magazine called the *Cooperative Commonwealth* hired him as a writer for forty dollars a week. Feeling rich, he sent gifts of money to his sisters, along with wishes for a merry Christmas. Unwilling to soften toward his mother even in this season of good cheer, he mailed a biting letter to her in California, where she and Leicester were visiting her brother. "Merry Christmas to you old dear—won't wish you Happy New Year because New Year is just one lurch nearer the grave and nothing to be happy over," he wrote. "Hope you have a priceless time."

When Bill Horne moved east, nearer his family, and Doodles Smith went to New York for music lessons, Ernest moved back in with Y. K. He visited Hadley in March, and she came to Chicago two weeks later, with some friends from St. Louis. One, Ruth Bradfield, called Ernest "a beautiful youth." The way he focused his attention on a person speaking to him "was immensely flattering," she noted. "He generated excitement because he was so intense about everything, about writing and boxing, about good food and drink. Everything we did took on new importance when he was with us."

Ernest had brought excitement into Hadley's lonely life. The two decided to marry at summer's end and move to Italy soon after. They would live on Hadley's trust fund, which paid her three thousand dollars a year, and Ernest's earnings from articles he would write for the *Toronto Star.* The editors were willing to pay him by the piece to be their first foreign correspondent. But most of the time, Ernest would be free to write as he wished. "The world's a jail," Hadley proclaimed, "and we're going to break it together."

Ernest admitted that he would go on loving Hadley "for a little while at least." He had begun to foresee the changes that marriage would bring, and to mourn the loss of fishing trips with his pals. A "guy loves a couple or three streams all his life and loves 'em better than anything in the world—falls in love with a girl and the goddam streams can dry up for all he cares," he lamented to Bill Smith. "Only the hell of it is that all that country has as bad a hold on me as ever."

Friends and family responded to the engagement with warmth and generosity. Grace Hemingway, hopeful that a wife would persuade Ernest to settle down and plan for the future, invited the couple to honeymoon at Windemere. Y. K. Smith insisted that they live in his house after they were married, free of charge, in a room with a four-poster bed. Then sometime during that summer of prolonged heat in Chicago, Ernest picked a fight with Y. K. He criticized Doodles's housekeeping and free and easy ways, and hinted that she paid too much attention to other men. Y. K. angrily withdrew his offer.

Except for this incident, the summer of 1921 passed happily. Hadley gave Ernest a new typewriter for his birthday, and soon September 3, their wedding day, arrived. They were married in Horton Bay, as far as possible from Hadley's lifelong home. "I was dull in St. Louis," she said. "Everything was dull in St. Louis."

The wedding made a vivid impression on Leicester, who sat in a front pew. The bride looked to him like an angel, although her thick hair was still damp from a swim, but the groom appeared nervous. Ernest's legs kept "moving from side to side as well as forward. His heavy white serge trousers seemed to have a serious case of shivers," Leicester observed. Hadley and Ernest exchanged their vows and joined their many guests to feast on fried chicken and a luscious cloud of a cake that took, in Leicester's opinion, far too long to be cut.

After two weeks alone at Windemere, nursing colds, Ernest and Hadley returned to Chicago, to a shabby apartment that they reached by climbing five flights of stairs. They were saving to go to Italy—until Sherwood Anderson convinced them that Paris was the place to be. Anderson had spent six months in the French capital and had fallen in love with it "wholeheartedly and without reservation." His dark eyes sparkled as he spoke of cafés where writers sat for hours, composing verses; he described gardens so exquisite they moved him to tears, streets lined with inviting little shops, and a vibrant night life. He mentioned the writers he had met, women and men who had abandoned their homelands to live in

Leicester Hemingway claimed his brother was a nervous groom, but both Ernest and Hadley radiate happiness in this wedding picture. From left to right are Carol, Ursula, Hadley, Ernest, Grace, Leicester, and Ed.

this stimulating place. He recalled Gertrude Stein, whose experiments in writing were inspired by abstract art, emphasizing sounds and forms, while the meaning was often obscure. He talked about Ezra Pound, who wrote poetry that relied on strong images for its beauty. Best of all, he said, a couple could live well in Paris on very little money.

Ernest and Hadley agreed that Paris would be their home. They booked passage on an old French ship, the *Leopoldina*, which was scheduled to sail from New York City during the second week of December. Sherwood Anderson gave them letters of introduction to his writer friends in Paris. And the night before they left Chicago, the Hemingways repaid his kindness by packing up all the canned food in their apartment and giving it to the Andersons.

FIVE

True Sentences

In 1921, at Christmastime, Ernest Hemingway found Paris to be "cold and damp but crowded, jolly and beautiful." He and Hadley moved into a small flat at 74, rue du Cardinal Lemoine. They slept in the ornate, old mahogany bed that filled the main room, and they shared a hall toilet with their neighbors on the fourth floor. The building sat next to the Bal Musette, a dance hall that was popular with the working men and women of the neighborhood. It was around the corner from the Café des Amateurs, which Hemingway considered a "sad, evilly run café where the drunkards of the quarter crowded together."

To work undisturbed, he rented a room on the top floor of a shabby hotel in the rue Mouffetard. Every morning, he climbed the six flights of stairs to his private space, built a fire in the fireplace, pulled a blue notebook from his desk drawer, and settled down to write. He practiced his art in the most basic way he knew, telling himself, "All you have to do is write one true sentence. Write the truest sentence that you know."

"It was easy then," he explained, "because there was always one true sentence that I knew or had seen or had heard someone say." He crafted

Waiters converse at a Paris café. The city in the 1920s soon looked much as it had before the war. "There are many black dresses, many armless sleeves," observed a travel writer. "But Paris in the springtime is still tempting."

paragraphs from these honest statements, making every word count. He believed that if he did his job right, then readers would understand the emotions that lay beneath the actions he described. Each day he stopped writing at a point when he knew what was coming next, so his pencil would be busy first thing the next morning.

For Ernest Hemingway, being a writer meant seeing, tasting, and doing. He sat in Paris cafés, observing the passing crowds. He danced with Hadley until the wee hours at the Bal Musette, and he chatted with strangers and new acquaintances. Hemingway picked up French as quickly as he had mastered Italian.

In late January, the Hemingways took off for Switzerland, which Ernest summed up as "a small, steep country, much more up and down than side-ways." He and Hadley learned to ski and spent hours hiking up the snowy alpine slopes and coasting down. When Ernest's battle-scarred right leg grew tired, they rode the hickory sleds called luges down steep, icy mountain roads. The thrill of the luge for Ernest was its speed. "You are sitting absolutely unsupported, only ten inches above the ice, and the road is feeding past you like a movie film," he told readers of the *Toronto Star.*

The owners of their small hotel fed the guests solid, nourishing meals. Ernest and Hadley fueled themselves on juicy roast beef, sausages slathered with mustard, enormous omelets, and big bowls of blueberries and whipped cream. Exhausted, they slept soundly each night under thick, feathery comforters, breathing the clean, chilled mountain air that poured in their open windows. Only one thing could have made the trip better for Ernest: sharing the fun with male companions. Bill Smith, Ted Brumback, and the others were on the far side of the ocean, so he wrote to his old friend from the hospital in Milan, Chink Dorman-Smith, and invited him to Switzerland. Chink, who had stayed in the army, was stationed in Ireland and could not get away.

Back in Paris, the Hemingways called on Sherwood Anderson's friends in the city's dynamic literary community. They met Sylvia Beach, the proprietor of Shakespeare and Company, a bookstore and rental library carrying literature printed in English. Books covered the shop's walls from floor to ceiling, and antique chairs tempted patrons to linger by the toasty wood-burning stove. Ernest found Beach to be warm and inviting as well. A native of Baltimore, she was a small woman with bobbed brown hair and alert, smiling dark eyes. "She was kind, cheerful and interested, and loved to make jokes and gossip," Hemingway said. "No one that I ever knew was nicer to me." Beach let the young writer check out as many books as he liked from the rental library, even though the deposit was more than he could afford. She said that he could pay her later, when he had the money.

In February 1922, Beach showed she was a woman of courage by publishing *Ulysses,* the second novel by the Irish writer James Joyce. Although *Ulysses* was destined to become one of the great books of the twentieth century, many readers of the 1920s found it indecent because it contained passages about sex. Publishing companies had refused to touch Joyce's book after the editors of the *Little Review,* an American journal, were found guilty of obscenity for printing an excerpt.

Hemingway understood the importance of Joyce's book and helped his new friend Beach find customers for it. Through his connections in the American press, he arranged to have forty copies of *Ulysses* smuggled into the United States and sent to people who valued good literature and freedom of expression, including certain booksellers and Sherwood Anderson. Hemingway would later meet the nearly blind Joyce, who was living in Paris with his wife and children.

Ernest and Hadley also visited author Gertrude Stein and her longtime companion, Alice B. Toklas. Paintings covered the walls of Stein's studio, which looked to the Hemingways like a room in a museum. Works by such recent masters as Gauguin, Matisse, and Toulouse-Lautrec hung beside canvases by Picasso and other up-and-coming artists.

Sylvia Beach stands in the doorway of her Paris bookshop, Shakespeare and Company.

Gertrude Stein holds
her little dog, Pepe.

The forty-eight-year-old Stein took a motherly interest in the aspiring writer. When she and Toklas went to see the Hemingways in their simple home, she sat her large body on the mahogany bed and read some of Ernest's stories. "There is a great deal of description in this," she said, "and not very good description. Begin over again and concentrate." Ernest felt a small shiver pass along his spine, because Stein's advice matched the goal that he had set for himself, to write simply and truthfully.

Stein rejected one story, titled "Up in Michigan," because of its sexual content. It was *inaccrochable*—"unhangable," she said. Like a painter whose picture cannot be hung because of what it depicts, Hemingway had created a story that the public would never see, she explained.

Another new acquaintance, the red-haired Ezra Pound, was a strange mix: gifted poet, outspoken anti-Semite, and generous friend. From his pen flowed both beautiful verses and hate-filled articles blaming the Jews for World War I. His friends tried to overlook the ugly side of Pound's character, because they had seen him help unknown writers achieve recognition, with no gain for himself. Hemingway viewed Pound's extreme hatred as irrational and he would come to see it as a sign of deteriorating mental health.

Pound delighted Hemingway by asking for boxing lessons, although it was soon clear that he would never be world champion. "He habitually leads with his chin and has the general grace of a crayfish," Hemingway remarked in a letter to Sherwood Anderson. "Pound sweats well, though, I'll say that for him." Yet with practice, Pound improved. He "developed a terrific wallop," Coach Hemingway proudly reported.

In April, the *Toronto Star* sent Ernest to Genoa, Italy, for three weeks, to cover an economic conference. Representatives of thirty-four nations were coming together around a great square table in the Palazzo San Giorgio, a thirteenth-century building that had long been a center of commerce. They planned to discuss rebuilding European economies that were damaged in the world war. The delegates arrived with high expectations, but they disagreed on key points and made little headway.

Hemingway reached Genoa, checked into his hotel, and had just relaxed in a hot bath when the copper water heater hanging near the tub blew up, shooting steam, scalding water, and shards of metal all over the room. The blast lifted Hemingway out of the bathtub and threw him against the door. It left him with an eight-inch gash on his right shin, a bruised hip, a sprained wrist, and a badly scraped palm. Tiny cuts on his arms and chest dripped blood. When he complained, the owner of the hotel told the wounded guest that he was lucky: Instead of griping, he should have been thankful he was alive!

Very soon, the reporters in Genoa went to work. Hemingway befriended Max Eastman, a writer covering the conference for the Communist journal *The Masses*. He compared Eastman to "a big, jolly, middle-western college professor." Hemingway, to Eastman, was "a modest and princely-mannered boy."

The princely boy had little understanding of economics. Instead, he reported from Genoa with a novelist's eye for conflict and character, describing heated disputes in the conference hall and people who caught his attention. Thanks to his reports, readers of the *Toronto Star* learned that Germany's chancellor, Joseph Wirth, looked "like a tuba player in a German band," whereas Soviet foreign minister Georgy Chicherin resembled "a country grocery storekeeper with a ragged indefinite beard." Two Russian secretaries with

Poet Ezra Pound furthered the careers of other writers, including Ernest Hemingway.

Hemingway compared Max Eastman to a college professor when the two met in 1922. Their second meeting, in 1937, would be less friendly.

The Soviet delegates to the 1922 conference stroll on a Genoa sidewalk. Georgy Chicherin, the man Hemingway described as a country grocer, is first on the left.

stylish bobbed hair were "far and away the best looking girls in the conference hall," Hemingway informed his readers.

He better understood the threat posed to freedom by the black-shirted Fascists who marched in the streets. Throughout the Italian countryside, armed Fascist squads had taken the law into their own hands. They preached an extreme form of nationalism in which individuals surrendered their will to the state; and they tolerated no opposing views. Hemingway called them "a brood of dragons' teeth" that made "no distinction between Socialists, Communists, Republicans or members of cooperative societies." Everyone came under their suspicion.

Hemingway went back to Italy in May, this time with Hadley, to show her where he had been during the war. The trip began with hiking in Switzerland, where the Hemingways met up with Chink Dorman-Smith, who was on furlough. Ernest and Chink had sturdy boots, but Hadley wore leather walking shoes. After two days on the steep, snow-covered terrain, she described herself as "a human blister," so the men carried her for the last stretch of the trek. Ernest and Hadley said good-bye to Dorman-Smith and took a train to Italy. After resting her feet, Hadley was ready to stroll through Milan and see the old building that had been the Red Cross hospital.

When Ernest learned that the Fascist leader, Benito Mussolini, was also in Milan, he used his press credentials to secure an interview. He met *"Il Duce,"* as Mussolini was called, in the offices of the *Popolo d'Italia,* the Fascist newspaper, and found him to be a "big, brown-faced man with a high forehead, a slow smiling mouth, and large, expressive hands." Mussolini spoke ominously, telling his interviewer, "We have enough force to overthrow any government that might try to oppose or destroy us." Hemingway wrote an account of the meeting and sent it off to the *Toronto Star.*

The next stop for Ernest and Hadley was Schio, where he pointed out the woolen mill that had been the Schio Country Club. For Ernest, the town that had felt so alive in wartime seemed quiet and small. The

Mussolini, his arms folded and head tilted to his left, stands with Fascists wearing uniforms and medals on an outdoor platform in Rome, in 1922.

mountains that had seen so many daring ambulance rescues appeared "rain-furrowed and dull."

They went to Fossalta, where Ernest had been sent by the Red Cross to open a canteen. There they discovered that ugly plaster houses had replaced the bombed-out rubble. Standing beside the Piave River, where Ernest had been shot, they saw no sign of the trenches that had cut into the landscape, just two new dwellings on the opposite bank. Ernest felt let down. "Chasing yesterdays is a bum show," he concluded. Returning to the scenes of past glory was "like going into the empty gloom of a theater where the charwomen are scrubbing."

In September, the *Toronto Star* dispatched Hemingway to war-torn Constantinople (today called Istanbul) to cover the closing events of the Greco-Turkish War. Since 1919, Turkey had been repelling Greek in-

Tall, pointed minarets rise above the rooftops of Constantinople.
From these towers, faithful Muslims are called to prayer.

vaders and was finally succeeding. This Muslim nation was also forcing many Christian civilians to resettle. Hadley insisted he stay home, because the Turkish capital was plagued by epidemics, but he went anyway, leaving behind an angry wife. Before packing his bags, he had agreed to report as well for the International News Service (INS), an agency that provided news stories to papers throughout the United States. He did this secretly, because his agreement with the *Toronto Star* barred him from reporting for anyone else.

The trip got off to a rough start when a Paris taxi driver dropped Hemingway's typewriter and broke it. Then, as soon as he reached Constantinople, he was swarmed by mosquitoes and came down with malaria, just as Hadley had feared. He combated the fever, chills, and aches with bitter-tasting quinine and despite his illness went out to report on everything he saw and experienced.

"Constantinople is noisy, hot, hilly, dirty, and beautiful," he wrote. Calls to prayer rang out from the minarets that arose everywhere, from dusty hillsides and from clusters of weathered tenements. Defeated Greek soldiers moved along the roads leading from the city in a long, weary stream. Some traveled on horseback, others trod along by foot, but all were "dirty, tired, unshaven, wind-bitten," Hemingway reported.

Eighteen days after arriving, Hemingway, too, headed for home. Before returning to Paris, he stopped in the Turkish city of Edirne, which was then known as Adrianople. It poured rain, turning the streets to mud and soaking the soldiers and uprooted civilians who packed the train station. Every room in the single hotel had been taken, but the French-speaking manager permitted Hemingway to sleep in her office with two American cameramen who were filming events in the region. The office looked clean enough, but as soon as the lights were off, lice swarmed all over the three men. This time, when Hemingway complained, the manager asked him, "It is better than sleeping in the road?"

Outside Adrianople, Hemingway came upon a sight he never would forget: Thousands of Christian refugees who had been ordered to evacuate Thrace, a region of southeastern Europe, were making their way along an old stone road in the rain. Carts, cattle, and worn-out human beings moved forward in a "never-ending, staggering march." Hunger pained every stomach; heavy bundles weighed down many backs. A single voice broke the marchers' silence. It belonged to a woman lying in one of the carts, giving birth. Her husband held a blanket above her as shelter from the downpour.

Ernest returned to Paris with his head shaved to rid him of lice, and necklaces of ivory and amber as peace offerings for Hadley, his Feather Puss or Feathercat. Distressed at his appearance but relieved to have him home, Hadley forgave him for going against her wishes. Ernest also had to appease his bosses at the *Toronto Star,* who had noticed similarities between the stories he sent them and INS reports in other papers. He apologized and promised never to double-cross the *Star* again. But in December, when the paper sent him to Lausanne, Switzerland, to cover another international conference, he reported not only for the INS but also for another organization, the Universal News Service. This time he varied his stories to disguise the fact that they had the same author.

It is amazing that with all this traveling, Ernest still found time to climb to his garret and write. Yet by the time Hadley joined him in Lausanne, stacks of unpublished stories and poems filled his desk drawers. He asked Hadley to bring them, so she packed up everything she found. When she reached Lausanne, though, she was in tears. She had given the suitcase containing the stories to a railroad porter in Paris, she said, and she never saw it again. Ernest begged her not to worry, because he kept carbon copies of all his writing, and those were still safe at home. No, no, Hadley said. She had packed the copies, too.

Ernest immediately caught a Paris-bound train, hardly believing that what Hadley told him could be true. "It was true all right," he later wrote, "and I remember what I did in the night after I let myself into the flat and found it was true." He never revealed just what it was he did, but he understood that he would have to start fresh as a writer. Just two stories survived: "Up in Michigan," which Gertrude Stein had rejected, and one called "My Old Man," set in the world of horseracing.

Hemingway began anew in Rapallo, Italy, in February 1923. He and Hadley went there to visit Ezra Pound and his wife, Dorothy, who had traded Paris's winter chill for the warm Italian coast. Palm trees grew in Rapallo, and a medieval castle sat on a spit of land in the bay, but the scenery failed to inspire Hemingway. He completed six short sketches exploring violence in the twentieth century for the *Little Review*. He based some of this writing on Chink Dorman-Smith's war stories and some on a newspaper account of the execution of six Greek cabinet ministers. He accomplished nothing else, though, and he feared that his writing life was finished. Then Hadley revealed some news Ernest found distressing: She was pregnant. It was even harder for Ernest to write when he worried about becoming a father at such a young age.

At this low point, he met Edward J. O'Brien, a poet from Boston with gentle blue eyes. O'Brien edited an annual collection of the best short stories of the previous year.

Hemingway still had a pair of good stories. With a careless air, he produced a creased copy of "My Old Man" and showed

A travel poster printed in French around 1920 calls Rapallo and the surrounding region the Italian Riviera.

it to O'Brien, who read the story and loved it. His yearly books contained only stories that had already been published in magazines, but he decided to make an exception. "My Old Man" would appear in *The Best Short Stories of 1923*.

The Hemingways also met Robert McAlmon, a California writer who had founded Contact Editions to publish books that might be too new and different for the old, established American publishers. McAlmon was handsome and witty, but some people found him cold and wary. In the spring of 1923, he took Ernest to Spain, paying all his expenses. Two

Artist Henry "Mike" Strater painted several portraits of
Ernest Hemingway, including this one from 1922 or 1923.

other Americans went with them: Henry (Mike) Strater, a painter the
Hemingways had met in Paris, and Bill Bird, a tall newspaperman whose
mind bubbled over with ideas. Bird had started the Three Mountains
Press to publish new editions of classical works. At Ezra Pound's urging,
he had agreed to publish modern writing as well.

Hemingway loved everything about Spain, from the heat of the golden
sun to the fragrance of grain growing in the countryside to the fountains
and palaces of the great promenades in Madrid. Yet traveling as McAlmon's guest made him ill at ease, and he reacted by demeaning his host.

When their train stopped beside a railroad flatcar bearing the rotting carcass of a dog, he made fun of McAlmon for turning away. Writers needed stamina, he said, to see and experience everything. He also mocked McAlmon's distaste for the bullfights, which both men witnessed for the first time. Bill Bird counseled Hemingway to curb his tongue, but the insults continued. Ernest Hemingway had to be the one in control, the strongest, and the most talented. If he felt threatened, he could be a vicious competitor.

Once back in Paris, however, good manners prevailed. Hemingway treated McAlmon kindly, and McAlmon offered to publish a small volume of Hemingway's work. The book would have to be slender, because Hemingway had only "Up in Michigan," "My Old Man," a new story about a married couple traveling in Italy called "Out of Season," and several poems. McAlmon considered Hemingway's fiction superior to his poetry, but he took everything.

During Hemingway's lifetime and in the years after his death, most readers have agreed with McAlmon. Hemingway lacked a poet's finely tuned ear for the music of language. Also, the depth of feeling that characterizes great poetry is missing from his verses. These lines are from an early poem named for a Paris neighborhood, "Montparnasse":

> There are never any suicides in the quarter among people one
>   knows . . .
> A Chinese boy kills himself and is dead.
> (they continue to place his mail in the letter rack at the Dome)
> A Norwegian boy kills himself and is dead.
> (no one knows where the other Norwegian boy has gone)
> They find a model dead
> alone in bed and very dead. . . .
> Every afternoon the people one knows can be found at the café.

For Hemingway the writer of fiction, there was more good news. Bill Bird had read his sketches of modern-day violence in the *Little Review*. He said that if Hemingway would complete several more vignettes like these, then the Three Mountains Press would issue them as a book.

To write more about violence, Hemingway needed material. He also wanted to see more bullfights. In July, he and Hadley went to Pamplona, where the festival of San Fermín featured the world's finest bullfighting. Their bus pulled into town at night, when bouncing strings of electric lights illuminated the square, dancers spun in the streets, and fireworks burst open overhead.

Their happy days in Pamplona began at dawn, when they watched the running of the bulls. The animals chosen for the day's fights were raced along the cobblestone streets to their pens at the Plaza de Toros, and young men showed off their bravery by running ahead of the galloping hooves. The Hemingways joined the revelers who danced, sang, and drank wine, day and night. And each afternoon, they watched the best matadors in Spain battle the bulls. Ernest found the violence he was looking for in the bullring. Five of the eight matadors who performed in Pamplona that July were gored during the week-long festival. "By God they have bullfights in that town!" he wrote to Bill Horne, his friend from Schio and Chicago.

Ernest and Hadley most admired Nicanor Villalta, a leggy, long-necked matador who faced the bulls with great bravery. They agreed that if they had a boy, they would name him after this lean, young wolf.

SIX

Becoming the Real Thing

John Hadley Nicanor Hemingway let out his first cry in a Toronto hospital on October 10, 1923. Hadley had insisted that her child be born in North America, where she felt surer of receiving good medical care. Ernest missed his son's birth, because he was in New York covering events for the *Toronto Star*. It cost more to live in Toronto than in Paris, so he had returned to full-time newspaper work. The *Star*'s city editor, Harry Hindmarsh, rode hard on the reporters working for him. Because Hemingway had lived in Europe and had two books coming out, Hindmarsh wanted to put him in his place. He kept Hemingway on the move, sending him to places like New York and northern Ontario, and gave the choice local assignments to other staffers.

The healthy baby thrived despite his father's travels, and soon his parents were calling him Bumby. When Bumby was a month old, he started to laugh, and Ernest admitted, "I am getting very fond of him."

He was less thrilled with life in Canada, because newspaper work left him no time to write. His colleague Morley Callaghan, then a college student working part-time for the *Star,* understood that Hemingway "was willing to be ruthless with himself or with anything or anybody that got in the way of the perfection of his work." Ernest and Hadley both missed the people and sights of Europe. "Our hearts are heavy, heavy," Hadley lamented, "just when we ought to be so happy." Toronto was a long way from Pamplona; although only a few months had passed since they had seen that sun-baked town, "It seems in a different century now," Ernest said.

Ernest's friends in Europe thought of him as well, because his books were published that fall in France. *Three Stories and Ten Poems* was a small blue paperback with the story and poem titles printed on the cover. Hemingway dedicated the book to Hadley, and in her personal copy he wrote, "The Feathercat, Her Book."

The volume published by Bill Bird's Three Mountains Press was called *in our time*. (Bird printed the titles of all the new work he published in lower-case letters.) The eighteen brief, numbered chapters expanded the study of modern-day violence that Hemingway had begun in the *Little Review* and proved that he could write powerful, pared-down prose.

Here is how he described the goring of two matadors in a single day:

> The first matador got the horn through his sword hand and the crowd hooted him out. The second matador slipped and the bull caught him through the belly and he hung onto the horn with one hand and held the other tight against the place, and the bull rammed him wham against the wall and the horn came out, and he lay in the sand, and then got up like crazy drunk and tried to slug the men carrying him away and yelled for his sword but he fainted.

In another vignette, Hemingway returned to the road outside Adrianople, where cavalrymen herded people, carts, and cattle along in the rain: "There was a woman having a kid with a young girl holding a blanket over her and crying. Scared sick looking at it." Because these pieces were fiction, Hemingway felt free to change details, to replace the woman's husband with a young girl. Some of the sketches, such as one about a veteran who contracts gonorrhea from a liaison in a taxi, went beyond what many people judged proper.

Hemingway watched eagerly for reviews of his books, but the press ignored them. He sent copies to Edmund Wilson, a man of letters who wrote about books for magazines and newspapers in the United States, and he kept searching for his name in print.

Just before Christmas, he made a quick trip to Oak Park to see his family, leaving Hadley and Bumby in Toronto. No arguments marred this visit. To Grace Hemingway, Ernest had changed; she thought he had grown "mature in judgment." She said, "You will never know the joy it is to a mother to find her son is a thoroughbred." Ernest privately gave Marcelline a copy of *Three Stories and Ten Poems,* but he mentioned nothing to his parents about his two books, knowing they would frown upon stories like "Up in Michigan." Afterward, from Toronto, he mailed them an order form for *in our time,* and they sent away for six copies.

Ernest resigned from the *Toronto Star* as of January 1, 1924, and he and Hadley went home to Paris with Bumby. Money was tighter for the Hemingways without his income from reporting, but they patched their

Alice B. Toklas and Gertrude Stein fuss over baby Bumby. Hadley and Ernest asked the two women to be their son's godmothers.

worn clothing, Ernest skipped lunch, and they made ends meet. They moved into a larger apartment that was next to a noisy sawmill, and Ernest wrote at the dining table. "Hemingway, in his loft above the carpenter's shop in the rue de Notre Dame des Champs with the wood dust floating in the shafts of light, could laugh," recalled his friend Archibald MacLeish. "He had whittled a new style for his time and he knew it." There were moments, though, when his happy mood turned to melancholy. "I've never seen a man go through the floor of despair as he did," added MacLeish, a poet who had given up a law career in Boston and moved to Paris with his wife, Ada, so both could write.

If Bumby's crying or the grinding of the machinery destroyed his concentration, Ernest carried his pencil and paper to a quiet café, the Closerie des Lilas. There, he could lose himself in his imagination. When he was writing a story about trout fishing in Michigan, the tables and people around him disappeared, and he felt as though he were wading in the water and casting his line. "When I stopped writing I did not want to leave the river where I could see the trout in the pool, its surface pushing and swelling smooth against the resistance of the log-driven piles of the bridge," he said.

He was testing a new way of constructing stories. He wanted to see what would happen if he left out some of the events in a character's past. Would they still leave an imprint on the story? Could they still affect the reader? This was why he never stated that the character fishing in this story was a soldier home from the war. He hoped this unwritten detail would add depth.

When Ford Madox Ford, a British novelist living in Paris, started a literary magazine, Ezra Pound persuaded him to make Hemingway the assistant editor. The three men had gathered in Pound's studio, where Hemingway danced and threw imaginary punches, like a boxer. "He's an experienced journalist," Pound told Ford, "and he's the finest prose stylist in the world."

Ford's magazine was called the *transatlantic review*. (Bill Bird suggested the lower-case letters.) Hemingway used his position to publish work by his friends, including Gertrude Stein and Donald Ogden Stewart, a writer of humorous stories who would find success penning scripts in Hollywood. Ford repelled Hemingway, however. Hemingway held his breath when standing next to Ford in his dirty clothes and hated looking at his stained mustache. After listening to Hemingway complain about Ford and threaten to embarrass him, Pound told his young friend to keep silent. He was never to treat Ford rudely, Pound said, and always to remember that he was a good writer. Ford was also a great admirer of Hemingway's fiction. "I did not read more than six words of his before I decided to publish everything that he sent me," Ford said.

Ford Madox Ford relaxes outdoors on a warm day in 1935. Ford recognized Hemingway's talent, but his careless hygiene repelled the younger writer.

The April 1924 issue of the *transatlantic review* included a new story by Ernest Hemingway, "Indian Camp." This story features the character Nick Adams, the hero of several later short works by Hemingway, among them "Fathers and Sons." Adams is an American of Hemingway's generation. His experiences differ in detail from his creator's, but many readers have thought that his emotional life mirrors Hemingway's. "Indian Camp" presents Nick as a boy accompanying his father, who is a doctor, to a Native American settlement. His father performs an emergency cesarean section, and Nick sees a baby born for the first time. Nick understands what is happening and is unafraid, but the woman's screams terrify her husband, who slits his own throat. Later, Nick asks his father why the man killed himself. "I don't know, Nick," his father says. "He couldn't stand things, I guess."

The same issue contained the first reviews of Hemingway's books. Readers of the *transatlantic* learned that the stories in *Three Stories and Ten Poems* displayed "a sensitive feeling for the emotional possibilities of a situation." They read that the short pieces making up *in our time* presented "moments when life is condensed and clean-cut and significant," distilled in "minute narratives that eliminate every useless word."

Edmund Wilson's review of both books appeared six months later in the *Dial,* the leading American literary journal of the 1920s. Wilson proclaimed that Hemingway's stories revealed "profound emotions and complex states of mind." He stated that *in our time* "has more artistic dignity than anything else about the period of the war that has as yet been written by an American."

Not everyone agreed. Bill Bird informed Ernest that someone in Oak Park named Hemingway had returned five copies of *in our time.* Ernest was used to his parents' unbending morals, but to have them reject his book in such a callous way offended him deeply. He immediately sent a letter to his family that ridiculed their safe, narrow taste in books. "I wonder what was the matter, whether the pictures were too accurate and the attitude toward life not sufficiently sentimentally distorted to please," he chided. "I have no inclination to defend my writing. All my thoughts and energies go to make it better and truer." He added that "a work of art that is really good never lacks for defenders, nor for people who hate it and want to destroy it."

The distance between Ernest and the Hemingways of Oak Park could be measured in attitudes as well as in miles. Hadley and Bumby had become his family. "As for Bumby, anything was all right as long as he was with his adored Papa," observed Sylvia Beach. "His first steps were to what he called 'Sylver Beach's.' I can see them, father and son, coming along hand in hand up the street."

Friends mattered, too. Ernest first met Harold Loeb, a Jewish writer from New York, at an afternoon tea hosted by Ford. Hemingway attended Ford's weekly teas in old sneakers and a patched jacket, whereas Loeb, who came from a wealthy family, always arrived well dressed. Loeb and his girlfriend, Kitty Cannell, often had dinner with Ernest and Hadley. Kitty felt sorry

The collage of newspaper clippings that decorated the cover of *in our time* reinforced the message that these stories dealt with timely topics.

for Hadley in her shabby dresses and gave her clothing and jewelry, but this put Ernest in a bad temper. He suspected that Kitty was finding fault with him as a husband. How much better it was when she gave the Hemingways a kitten! They loved the little cat and named it Feather Puss.

Boni and Liveright, a publishing house in New York, had accepted Loeb's first novel, *Doodab*. When a talent scout for Boni and Liveright came to Paris to hunt for new books to publish, Loeb gave him Hemingway's new stories. Then he and Hemingway kept their fingers crossed.

But Ernest Hemingway could never sit still and wait. No sooner was he in one place than he itched to be somewhere else. As the summer of 1924 approached, he longed to be in Spain. He had raved to so many people about Pamplona that when he and Hadley returned there in June, a whole group of friends trailed along. Chink Dorman-Smith went, and so did Donald Ogden Stewart, the humorist; Robert McAlmon went, as well as Bill Bird and his wife, Sally. (Bumby remained in Paris, in a babysitter's care.) One new friend who made the trip was the American writer John Dos Passos. A graduate of Harvard University and the son of a wealthy lawyer, he had published two novels inspired by his experiences in the war, *One Man's Initiation—1917: A Novel* and *Three Soldiers*. Dos Passos loved Spain as much as Hemingway did.

For Ernest, this trip was a test of bravery. He kept track of how each friend reacted to the bullfights: Dorman-Smith detested the killing of horses but liked the technical aspects of bullfighting; one trip to the bullring was enough for Sally Bird. "Ernest was somebody you went along with, or else," said Donald Stewart, who happily discovered that he liked bullfighting almost as much as his friend Ernest did. On the last morning of the fiesta, Donald and Ernest took part in the amateur matches held before the day's professional fights. Padding covered the sharp tips of the bulls' horns, and matadors stood by to offer advice, but entering the ring with these mighty, volatile beasts was dangerous nonetheless. A bull charged Stewart and threw him into the air, cracking two of his ribs, but he landed on his feet, beaming with delight. "I had shown I could take

A bullfighter pushes a sword deep into the shoulder of a bull as a crowd watches in Seville, Spain.

it," he said. "Ernest clapped me on the back, and I felt as though I had scored a winning touchdown."

Hemingway "had an extraordinary dedication to whatever his interest was for the moment," Dos Passos observed. Whether it was bullfighting or skiing or fishing, "He stuck like a leech till he had every phase of the business in his blood."

In December, the Hemingways took off for Schruns, a town in Austria, to spend the winter skiing. This time, Bumby came along. The Hotel Taube, where they stayed, was cheap and pretty, with a piano for Hadley to play and a bowling alley where Ernest relaxed at night. He made up for his missed lunches by downing heaping plates of meat in gravy, potatoes, and plum pudding. "Every meal time was a great event," he said.

One evening, upon returning from a long day of skiing, he found telegrams waiting for him from Donald Stewart and Harold Loeb, who were both in New York. They had written with big news: Loeb's publishers, Boni and Liveright, wanted to bring out his stories as a book. At first, Ernest thought his friends were joking, but then a third telegram came from Horace Liveright himself. Liveright wanted to publish this book as well as the next two that Hemingway wrote. Hemingway was so excited that he barely slept that night.

The book would be published in the fall. That spring, in Paris, Hemingway was drinking with some English friends in a bar one night when he met another writer, F. Scott Fitzgerald. Fitzgerald lived abroad, but he captured American life in the 1920s, especially among the wealthy, in novels such as *The Great Gatsby*. Hemingway admired Fitzgerald's talent, which he called "as natural as the pattern that was made by the dust on a butterfly's wings." But like those beautiful wings, Fitzgerald's gift was fragile. As their friendship developed, Hemingway came to realize that alcoholism threatened Fitzgerald's future as a writer. Also, his wife, Zelda, seemed jealous of his work. She pressured her husband to attend parties and drink, and her face glowed in triumph when he became too drunk to write.

Fitzgerald recognized Hemingway's promise as well. He informed his

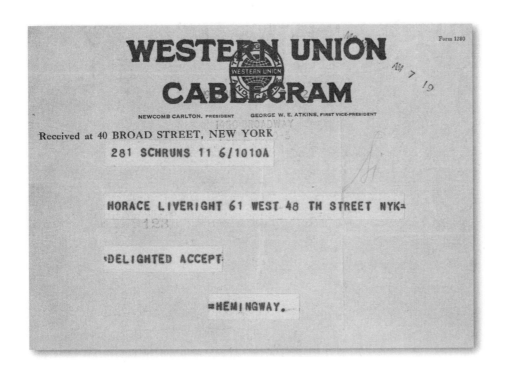

From Austria, Hemingway sent Horace Liveright this cable accepting Liveright's offer to publish *In Our Time*. Sending a telegram by transatlantic cable was the fastest way to communicate between Europe and the United States in the early twentieth century.

Hemingway's friend
F. Scott Fitzgerald, as
he looked in the 1920s.

editor in New York, Maxwell Perkins, that a young man named Ernest Hemingway had written some remarkable stories for the *transatlantic review,* and that he had a brilliant future. "He's the real thing," Fitzgerald stressed. Perkins worked for the distinguished publishing house Charles Scribner's Sons.

During the twenties many young people questioned the values of their parents' generation. In the United States, where alcoholic beverages had been outlawed, they defiantly drank gin in the illegal bars known as speakeasies. They danced to jazz bands and experimented with sex. Young women showed they were free thinkers by cutting their hair and smoking. Gertrude Stein called the men and women who came of age in this decade the "lost generation." Not only had millions of the boys in this age group literally been lost in World War I, but also the young of both sexes bore psychological scars from living through the war. They drank to numb their pain, and they lacked respect for social institutions.

The English couple who drank with Hemingway on the night he met Fitzgerald were the kind of people Stein had in mind. The woman, Duff Twysden, was twice married and twice divorced. Her second husband had been a baronet, which made her Lady Twysden. She drank heavily, laughed loudly, and wore a man's hat to show off her nonconformity. Her male companion, Pat Guthrie, was her cousin as well as her lover.

When summer returned, and Ernest and Hadley made their annual trip to Pamplona, Twysden and Guthrie came along. Donald Stewart, Harold Loeb, and Bill Smith, Ernest's old friend from Michigan, completed the party. The carefree happiness of previous summer excursions was gone, though. The trip was to begin with a week of fishing near the Spanish town of Burguete, but logging had filled the stream with debris and caused most of the trout to die. "Made me feel sick," Ernest said.

Pamplona, too, had changed for the worse. Wealthy American tourists had discovered the festival of San Fermín; the huge demand for food, hotels, and bullfight tickets had driven up prices. Bill Smith outshone Ernest in the amateur bull matches, which robbed them of enjoyment as far as Ernest was concerned. But more complicated jealousies also marred the celebration. Before going to Pamplona, Twysden and Loeb had carried on a brief love affair. When everyone drank, anger surfaced, and people traded insults. "One night there was almost a fistfight between Ernest and Harold Loeb," Donald Stewart remembered. "The fun was going out of everybody."

When the festival ended, Ernest and Hadley parted from the others and went to Madrid for more bullfighting. They stayed in the Pension Aguilar, a hotel where matadors lodged, and they met some of these courageous men. Cayetano Ordóñez, one of Spain's great bullfighters, honored Hadley by dedicating the killing of a bull to her. Ordóñez sliced an ear from the bull and presented it to Hadley; she wrapped it in a handkerchief and saved it in her bureau drawer.

Ernest Hemingway left Pamplona without the happy memories of earlier years, but he came away with something better: the idea for a novel. He wrote furiously, as he and Hadley traveled in other parts of Spain, often staying awake until three or four in the morning. He wrote in small notebooks, and by mid-August, when he returned to Paris, he had filled 250 pages.

He wrote about Jake Barnes, an American journalist living in Paris. A war wound has left Barnes unable to enjoy a physical relationship with the woman he loves, Lady Brett Ashley. Readers never learn the exact nature of Barnes's injury, but his alienation may be psychological as well. Like most of the characters, Ashley is a thinly disguised version of a real person—in this case, Lady Duff Twysden. Ashley is engaged to the alcoholic Mike Campbell, but she has an affair with Barnes's friend Robert Cohn, a wealthy American Jew. This short romance is merely a fling for Ashley, but Cohn becomes infatuated with her.

The friends go to Pamplona for the festival of San Fermín. They witness bullfights, and Hemingway writes from experience about the things they hear and see: the roar of the crowd in the Plaza de Toros, the graceful movements of a good matador, mules hauling a dead bull from the

Ernest, Hadley, and friends
savor café life in Pamplona,
in July 1925. Ernest sits
next to Duff Twysden.

ring. Like Hadley, Brett Ashley receives a bull's ear from the handsome matador who killed the bull.

Meanwhile, tensions build. The others resent Cohn's presence because he refuses to see that he has no future with Ashley, and because of his faith. They reveal their prejudice through anti-Semitic remarks. Everyone drinks to excess. "Under the wine I lost the disgusted feeling and was happy. It seemed they were all such nice people," Jake says. Jake drinks to hide from the truth; his friends drink for reasons of their own.

The alcohol gives Mike Campbell courage, and he attacks Robert

Cohn like a bull charging a steer. "Don't you know you're not wanted? I know when I'm not wanted. Why don't you know when you're not wanted?" Campbell asks. "What if Brett did sleep with you? She's slept with lots of better people than you."

Ashley betrays both rivals by leaving Pamplona with the gallant matador. The festival ends, and Barnes relaxes alone at San Sebastian, on the Spanish coast—until Ashley sends him a telegram asking for help. She is stranded; the bullfighter has left her in a Madrid hotel without any moncy.

Barnes hurries to Madrid and pays Ashley's bill. Over a lunch that includes several bottles of wine, Ashley resigns herself to the future she has been trying to escape, the ordinary adult life of a wife and mother. Afterward, as the two tour Madrid in a taxi, she gives voice to her regrets. "Oh, Jake," she says. "We could have had such a damned good time together."

Here Hemingway paused to decide how Jake would reply. Should he say, "It's nice as hell to think so"? Or "Isn't it nice to think so"? The exhausted author knew he would come up with something better, but for the moment he jotted, "The End . . . Paris—Sept. 21—1925."

SEVEN

Generations

Hemingway considered calling his novel *The Lost Generation,* remembering how Gertrude Stein's words had inspired him. But he rejected that title, because although he had written about one generation, he had portrayed aspects of human nature that remain the same in every era. After much thinking and searching, he found words that describe the cyclical nature of life in the book of Ecclesiastes, in the Bible: "One generation passeth away, and another generation cometh; but the earth abideth forever. The sun also ariseth, and the sun goeth down, and hasteth to his place where he arose." Hemingway called the book *The Sun Also Rises.*

He made the perfect choice, in Sylvia Beach's opinion. "I think Hemingway's titles should be awarded first prize in any contest," she commented. "Each of them is a poem, and their mysterious power over readers contributes to Hemingway's success. His titles have a life of their own, and they have enriched the American vocabulary."

He also settled on the right words to end his book—Jake Barnes's reply to Brett Ashley's wistful comment about the happy life they might have shared. "Isn't it pretty to think so?" Barnes asks, summing

Ava Gardner and Tyrone Power starred as Jake Barnes and Lady Brett Ashley in the 1957 film adaptation of *The Sun Also Rises.*

up the reluctance of Ashley and others like her to face life realistically.

As Hemingway put the final touches on his novel in Paris, his story collection was coming off the press in the United States. Called *In Our Time,* with the words capitalized, the book published by Boni and Liveright contained fourteen stories. They included "Soldier's Home," the story about Harold Krebs, the Oklahoma Marine traumatized by the war, and "Indian Camp," in which the young Nick Adams encounters birth and death. Adams reappears as a young man in several other stories— breaking up with a girl named Marjorie in one, discussing books with a friend named Bill in another, and catching rides on freight trains in a third. The book also included Hemingway's sketches of modern violence, placed so that each one preceded a longer story.

Hemingway divided the longest story, "Big Two-Hearted River," into Parts I and II. This was the story about fishing in Michigan that he had composed at the Closerie des Lilas. In Part I, Nick Adams gets off a train in Seney and discovers that fire has destroyed the small backwoods town. (Although fires commonly burned the forests around Seney, the damage that Hemingway described was fictional.) Nick hikes to the green banks of the river, sets up camp, cooks a meal over an open fire, and falls asleep in his tent. In Part II, Nick spends the next day fishing for trout. He seeks shadowy sections of the water and holes in the riverbed, places where he knows he'll find fish. He stays away from the deep swamp that hovers on the edge of his field of vision. The thought of "wading with the water deepening up under his armpits, to hook big trout in places impossible to land them" repels him. "In the swamp fishing was a tragic adventure."

This story describes simple actions but suggests a complex mental state. Hemingway's methodical prose, in which one short declarative sentence follows another, matches Nick's need for order: "Nick had one good trout. He did not care about getting many trout. Now the stream was shallow and wide. There were trees along both banks." Laid down in this way, the words have a numbing effect, just as the rituals of fishing seem to prevent Nick from thinking or feeling too much. Readers suspect Nick has suffered psychological shock, and the fishing trip is an effort to cope.

Readers often sense as well that the landscape of "Big Two-Hearted River" symbolizes Nick's state of mind. Hiking from the charred region to the green riverside is like moving from pain toward healing. The swamp may stand for the trauma that Nick is not ready to face. Some critics have even suggested that the entire fishing trip takes place in Nick's imagination.

Reviews of *In Our Time* appeared in the press soon after its publication. One critic praised Hemingway's "lyricism, aliveness and energy." A writer for the *New York Times* noted the stories' "lean, pleasing, tough resilience." More than one reviewer likened the writing to Sherwood Anderson's. This bothered Hemingway, who had worked so hard to develop a style all his own. The more he thought about these comparisons, the angrier he became.

Anderson, too, had just published a book, a novel called *Dark Laughter*. He had broken from the simple approach that gave *Winesburg, Ohio* its haunting beauty. Influenced by James Joyce's *Ulysses,* he produced impressionistic prose that went inside his characters' heads to record their random thoughts.

Anderson had begun his novel with these lines:

> Bruce Dudley stood near a window that was covered with flecks of paint and through which could be faintly seen, first a pile of empty boxes, then a more or less littered factory yard running down to a steep bluff, and beyond the brown waters of the Ohio River. Time very soon now to push the windows up. Spring would be coming soon now.

It amazed Hemingway, who disliked the book, to see it praised in the press. One reviewer even called Anderson "America's most interesting writer."

Determined to have that title for himself, Hemingway dashed off a short novel of his own called *The Torrents of Spring*. It was clear from the very first page that Hemingway intended to poke fun at Anderson's writing.

> Yogi Johnson stood looking out of the window of a big pump-factory in Michigan. Spring would soon be here. Could it be that what this writing fellow Hutchinson had said, "If winter comes can spring be far behind?" would be true again this year? Yogi Johnson wondered.

To show the world that he was a better writer than Sherwood Anderson, Ernest decided to send *The Torrents of Spring* to his publisher. Hadley and John Dos Passos tried hard to change his mind. It would be smarter to follow *In Our Time* with a good, serious novel rather than one that simply showed off his cleverness, they argued. Besides, Sherwood Anderson had been kind to the Hemingways, and this was a cruel way to pay him back.

Ernest, who had to be the best, refused to listen. He sent *The Torrents of Spring* to Horace Liveright, who immediately rejected it. In this way, Hemingway freed himself from his contract with Boni and Liveright. He then sent the manuscript to F. Scott Fitzgerald's editor, Maxwell Perkins of Charles Scribner's Sons, a more prestigious firm, and Perkins agreed to publish it. Soon afterward, Hemingway sent Perkins *The Sun Also Rises*.

Scribner's released both books in 1926, with very different results. *The Torrents of Spring* sold a small number of copies and ended Hemingway's friendship with Sherwood Anderson. *The Sun Also Rises* established Ernest Hemingway as an important name in literature. The American writer Conrad Aiken, reviewing *The Sun Also Rises,* praised Hemingway's "understanding and revelation of character which approaches the profound." He observed, "When one reflects on the unattractiveness, not to say the sordidness, of the scene, and the (on the whole) gracelessness of the people, one is all the more astonished at the fact that Mr. Hemingway should have made them so moving."

Once again, though, Ernest Hemingway felt the sting of his family's rejection. It was a "doubtful honor," his mother declared, to have written "one of the filthiest books of the year." Grace Hemingway had skipped her book club's discussion of *The Sun Also Rises,* because she "could not face being present." Her comments made Ernest so angry that he waited more than a month before responding. When he did reply, he launched a counterattack, informing his mother that the actions described in his novel were much like "the real inner lives of some of our best Oak Park families." There was just one difference: "You must remember that in such a book all the worst of the people's lives is displayed while at home there is a very lovely side for the public and the sort of thing of which I have had some experience in observing behind closed doors."

Ernest's father, too, made his disapproval known. "I shall trust your future books will have a different sort of subject matter," he wrote. "You have such a wonderful ability and we want to be able to read and ask others to enjoy your works." Before closing his letter, Ed Hemingway mentioned hearing rumors about "a serious domestic trouble." Was it true, he wanted to know, "that you and Hadley have had a break"?

It was true. As Hemingway was to reflect later in life, "All things truly wicked start from innocence."

The trouble began innocently enough in December 1925, when he,

Hadley, Bumby, and Ernest Hemingway enjoy the mountain air in Schruns, Austria.

Hadley, and Bumby went back to Schruns, Austria, for skiing. Hadley's friend Pauline Pfeiffer joined them at Christmas. A petite, dark-haired, fashionable American, Pauline was an assistant editor at *Paris Vogue* magazine. As she helped Hadley take care of Bumby and talked about books with Ernest, Hadley's happy married life—and her husband—began to look very attractive to Pauline, more so every day. For Ernest, too, feelings of friendship turned into something more.

Pauline returned to Paris in January, a few weeks before Ernest planned to sail to New York to meet with his publishers. When Ernest reached the French capital, en route to his ship, he and Pauline began an affair. In March, when his trip was over and he stepped ashore again in Europe, he could have gone directly to Austria, where Hadley waited. Instead, he spent two days with Pauline, resuming their romance. He chose a secret name for her, Pilar, after the Virgin of Pilar, the patron saint of Aragon, in northeast Spain.

Seeing Hadley at last, as she watched his train pull in at Schruns, stirred up love and remorse in Ernest's heart. "I wished I had died before I ever loved anyone but her," he confessed. "She was smiling, the sun on her lovely face tanned by the snow and sun, beautifully built, her hair red gold in the sun, grown out all winter awkwardly and beautifully, and Mr. Bumby standing with her, blond and chunky and with winter cheeks."

He did his best to forget Pauline, but when the Hemingways went home to Paris, "the other thing started again," Ernest said. Hadley learned about "the other thing"—the affair—in early May. She wept, and Ernest despaired. "I like to think about death and the various ways of dying," he wrote in his journal. He decided that dying while asleep would be the ideal way to go; jumping off an ocean liner at night and disappearing into the deep might be second best.

In September, Hadley offered the lovers a deal. If they still felt the same about each other after spending a hundred days apart, then she would grant Ernest a divorce. Pauline sailed to the United States, to spend the hundred days in Piggott, Arkansas, with her well-to-do family, and Ernest stayed in Paris, in a chilly one-room apartment. He took care of Bumby while Hadley went to Chartres, a French town with a great cathedral, to spend some time alone, thinking. He

In Schruns, Hemingway locks arms with John Dos Passos, to his left, and Gerald Murphy, a wealthy American artist whom he also befriended. Murphy thought Hadley was "miscast" as the wife of a successful writer and advised Ernest to separate from her "cleanly and sharply."

told Hadley she was "the best and truest and loveliest person that I have ever known," but on January 8, 1927, he met Pauline's ship at Cherbourg, France, one hundred seven days after she had left.

Ernest was skiing in Gstaad, Switzerland, with Pauline and her sister, Virginia (Jinny), when his divorce became final. He signed over to Hadley all his earnings from *The Sun Also Rises*. "It is the only thing that I who have done so many things to hurt you can do to help you," he told her, "and you must let me do it." The royalties, or earnings, for *The Sun Also Rises* amounted to between fifteen and thirty cents for every copy sold. Sales totaled twelve thousand copies by February 1927 and continued to be brisk. "The Sun has risen," Maxwell Perkins happily reported, "and is rising steadily." Thus, Hadley received a sizable income from the book.

Ernest Hemingway and the woman who became his second wife, Pauline Pfeiffer. Hadley denied that ambition led Ernest to divorce her. He "fell very hard in love with Pauline," she said, and added that the divorce caused him "deep remorse."

Wedding gifts of cash from Pauline's wealthy relatives made up for Ernest's financial loss. He and Pauline were married on May 10, 1927, in a Catholic church in Paris. Pauline had been raised in the Catholic faith, and Ernest claimed that he had received a Catholic baptism while in the hospital in Milan.

The couple honeymooned at the seacoast in southern France, where Ernest produced one of his finest short stories, "Hills Like White Elephants." Because he limited most of the action to dialogue, this story resembles a scene from a play. A young man—an American—and a young woman called Jig wait for a train in the Ebro River Valley of Spain. They sit at a table outside a café and drink beer and Anis del Toro, a licorice-flavored liqueur. The young man pressures Jig to have an operation, but she is undecided. She remarks that the distant hills look like white

Newlyweds Ernest and Pauline Hemingway
visit the beach at San Sebastian, Spain.

elephants. "They were white in the sun and the country was brown and
dry," Hemingway wrote.

In this story, he masterfully applies his "theory of omission," leaving
out key information that is nevertheless conveyed to the reader. The couple never uses the word "abortion," but clearly this is the operation being
discussed. Hemingway never describes how the characters say their
words, whether they shout, cry, whisper, plead, or speak angrily or sar-

castically. Yet there is no doubt that this is an emotional conversation, and because of Hemingway's skill, Jig's final words inflict a viper's bite: "There's nothing wrong with me. I feel fine."

"Hills Like White Elephants" is also rich in symbolism. The expression "white elephant," for example, can refer to a useless or unwanted object. This may be how one or both partners view the baby.

One small mishap marred the seaside honeymoon: Ernest cut his foot on a rock while swimming. The wound festered and swelled, forcing him to spend ten days in bed after returning to Paris in June. By July, the infection had cleared, and he headed for Pamplona with Pauline. While traveling that summer, he took care of a duty he had been avoiding: telling his family that he had divorced Hadley and married again. His mother's shame about his work had made him "shut up like a hermit crab," and he had written nothing to his parents in nine months.

The divorce "was entirely my fault and it is no one's business," he explained to his father. "I will never stop loving Hadley nor Bumby nor will I cease to look after them. I will never stop loving Pauline Pfeiffer to whom I am married." Before closing, he added, "You cannot know how it makes me feel for Mother to be ashamed of what I know as sure as you know there is a God in heaven is *not to be ashamed* of."

Ernest knew the value of his work, even if his parents did not. Within a few months he had finished enough stories for another book, which was published by Scribner's in 1927. Hemingway called this collection *Men Without Women,* because the stories featured men filling traditionally male roles or distanced emotionally from women. The book contained "Hills Like White Elephants" as well as tales of bullfighters, soldiers, boxers, and hit men.

Some critics praised the new book. The writer Dorothy Parker, reviewing *Men Without Women* for the *New Yorker* magazine, applauded Hemingway's skill at paring away details. "The simple thing he does looks so easy to do," she acknowledged, but writers who followed his example failed to match his achievement. Other reviewers objected to Hemingway's focus on masculinity. "The greatest writers lay no stress upon sex one way or the other," commented the British author Virginia Woolf.

Ernest and Pauline are among the crowd enjoying a bullfight in Pamplona in 1927. Ernest leans forward for a better look, and Pauline sits to his right, wearing a beret.

"The critic is not reminded as he reads them that he belongs to the masculine or the feminine gender."

Increasingly, Hemingway would be put down for presenting an exaggerated image of manliness in his writing and in his life. Although he did make a show of courage and pursued a number of the activities described in his stories, some of the credit—or blame—for this perception belonged to the press. Journalists not bothering to get their facts straight reported that Hemingway had been a high school football star and a boxer, that he had been wounded while fighting with the Italian army, and that he was an expert skier and a semiprofessional bullfighter.

Ernest Hemingway had become a celebrity, and everything that happened to him made news. The press even reported on an accident that occurred after a night of drinking, when he woke up and went into the bathroom. Half asleep, he pulled the chain that opened the skylight in the ceiling—only to have the whole window fall down on him. As blood poured from a deep gash in his forehead, Pauline phoned Archibald MacLeish, who hailed a taxi and took Ernest to a hospital. There, doctors closed his wound with nine stitches.

Having friends like the MacLeishes, Sylvia Beach, Gertrude Stein, and John Dos Passos enriched Hemingway's life in Paris, but the time had come to move on. For one thing, Ernest wished to distance himself from Hadley, who planned to remain in the city. For another, Pauline was pregnant, and like Hadley, she wanted her child born in an American hospital.

On March 17, 1928, with his forehead still healing, Ernest left Paris with Pauline and sailed west across the Atlantic to spend several months in Key West, Florida, the tiny island at the southeastern tip of the United States. Dos Passos had landed there a few years earlier, while on a hitchhiking trip. He had told Ernest and Pauline about swimming in deep blue water, smelling the Gulf Stream on the breeze, and drinking good Spanish wine in the island's small restaurants.

In the sunny, relaxed atmosphere of Key West, Hemingway soon collected a new group of friends. Bra Saunders was a fishing guide who skillfully navigated the waters surrounding south Florida. Joe Russell owned a bar called Sloppy Joe's, where Hemingway chatted with locals and drank rum smuggled in from Cuba. Charles Thompson's family owned several island businesses, including a hardware store, a fishing-tackle shop, and a cigar-box factory. Thompson taught Hemingway to fish the coastal waters for red snapper and tarpon, and in April Hemingway caught the biggest tarpon landed in Key West that season, one weighing sixty-three pounds.

Hemingway had his picture taken while the wound to his forehead was still fresh. The scar caused by this injury would be visible for the rest of his life.

Also in April, Grace and Ed Hemingway visited Key West. They had invested in Florida real estate and had come to see their property. Like thousands of Americans in the 1920s, they bought land in the Sunshine State, sight unseen, hoping to earn big money. They believed ads promising that every dollar invested "will double in value before you know it." With more and more northerners making Florida a warm winter vacationland, many speculators did earn high returns in the early 1920s. But others were taken in by shady dealers who sold them deeds to swampland, or saw their profits wiped out in 1926 by a strong hurricane that left hundreds of Floridians dead and thousands homeless. Suddenly, the value of land in Florida plummeted.

Financial worries made Ed Hemingway tired, old, and prone to tears. Diabetes had caused him to grow thin, and he confided to his son that he felt pain in his heart. Anyone seeing him with Grace Hemingway might not have believed that the two were husband and wife. Ernest's mother

With Captain Joe Russell, Ernest shows off his catch.

A vacationer relaxes under one of Key West's palm trees in 1926.

appeared hefty, healthy, and expensively dressed, as always. She recently had taken up oil painting.

Other guests followed: John Dos Passos, Bill and Katy Smith, and Waldo Peirce, a burly artist from Maine whom Hemingway had met in Paris. "Hem always did have a gang of people with him," Dos Passos recalled. Dos Passos called him Hem, but Hemingway had adopted another nickname, Papa, and he encouraged his friends to use it.

Papa Hemingway took his friends out in a small boat to fish the shallow waters around the island chain known as the Keys. He hired Bra Saunders to take them to the Dry Tortugas, tiny islands seventy miles to the west, to try for bigger fish. There, Peirce aroused Hemingway's envy by hooking a six-foot tarpon. Dos Passos liked the fishing well enough, but he much more enjoyed meeting Katy Smith, his future wife.

Hemingway fished and relaxed with friends in the afternoon and evening, but he reserved his mornings for work. He had started another

Ed Hemingway visits Key West. Ernest would never see his father again.

novel—an important one—based on his experiences in the Great War. By May, when he and Pauline left Key West, he had written more than a hundred pages.

They drove to Piggott, Arkansas, in a yellow Ford that was a gift from Pauline's rich uncle, Gus Pfeiffer. On June 17, they moved on to Kansas City, where Pauline had chosen to have her baby, to await the big event. Eleven days later, Patrick Hemingway was born. "Patrick is like a bull, bellows like a bull too," Ernest observed.

Father, mother, and baby returned to Piggott as soon as Pauline was well enough to travel, but the summer heat and Patrick's crying drove Ernest "bug house" and kept him from working. "I must write this book and not just write it, which alone is hard enough to do—but make it good," he vowed. In late July, he met up with his old friend Bill Horne in

Kansas City, and the two drove west, to fish in the trout streams of the Bighorn Mountains. Ernest felt that he had escaped from the trap of family life, at least for a while, and he hoped to find the conditions that would allow him to write.

Ernest and Bill settled at a dude ranch in Sheridan, Wyoming. As in Key West, Ernest wrote in the morning and fished in the afternoon. By August 18, when Pauline joined him, he had just thirty pages left to write. Four days later, he finished the book. With Jinny Pfeiffer caring for Patrick in Piggott, Ernest and Pauline toured the West by car, venturing as far as the Idaho border. They talked about the future and decided to make their home in Key West, where lime, mango, and avocado trees stayed green all year and businesses closed for an afternoon siesta.

In October, they picked up Patrick in Arkansas, drove to Key West, and moved into a big, white house that Charles Thompson and his wife, Lorine, had found for them to rent. Ernest's sister Sunny arrived after Thanksgiving to help type the final draft of his book.

But before he could sit down to work, Ernest went to New York to pick up five-year-old Bumby, who was sailing from France for a visit. An ocean separated Ernest from his older son, but he remained a devoted father to Bumby. He met the boy's ship, and on December 6 the pair boarded a Florida-bound train. At the stop in Trenton, New Jersey, a railroad worker gave Ernest a telegram. It was from his sister Carol, informing him that their father had died.

What to do? Ernest placed Bumby in a Pullman porter's care and caught an overnight train to Chicago. He went straight to Oak Park, and there he learned that Ed Hemingway had used a Civil War rifle inherited from his father to shoot himself in the head.

EIGHT

Dangerous Game

The crack of that fatal gunshot echoed in Hemingway's skull. In the weeks following his father's suicide, he struggled to make sense of this violent final act. "My father was a coward," he concluded. "He shot himself without necessity." Dr. Hemingway had lost most of his money in bad Florida investments, leaving his widow frightened about the future. Grace Hemingway rented rooms and gave voice and painting lessons to bring in cash. Although Ernest no longer felt close to his mother and occasionally ranted about her to his friends, he promised to send her a hundred dollars a month for as long as she lived.

He asked for the gun his father had used to take his own life. Grace sent it to him in a crate that also held some of her paintings and a chocolate cake, which had grown moldy by the time it reached Key West. Ernest could keep the gun only for a while, his mother said, because Leicester had asked for it too.

There is no convenient time for death or grieving, and Ernest coped with his loss while laboring on his new novel. He spent long hours revising the first draft by hand and passed along finished sections to Sunny or Pauline for typing. He called this new novel *A Farewell to Arms,* borrowing the title of a poem from the 1500s by an English writer, George Peele. Peele's poem concerns an aging knight who turns away from warring ways to lead a peaceful life.

Hemingway's novel follows Frederic Henry, an American ambulance volunteer in Italy during World War I, who makes a similar choice. At first, stationed in the town of Gorizia, Frederic knows only a "false feeling of soldiering." He watches the movement of troops from a window, and he compares distant flashes of nighttime artillery fire to something beautiful and familiar, "summer lightning." His first true experience of war comes while waiting out a battle in a dugout with other drivers. A high riverbank protects the volunteers from rifle and machine-gun fire but not from shelling. When an Austrian mortar shell explodes nearby, Frederic's leg is badly wounded and requires surgery. He is transferred to a hospital in Milan, where he falls in love with an English nurse who has also volunteered to aid the Italians, Catherine Barkley.

Until this point, Frederic's adventure closely follows his creator's. Once he falls in love with Catherine, though, their courses diverge. Catherine becomes pregnant; Frederic returns to the front in time to witness the disastrous Battle of Caporetto, in which German and Austrian forces broke through the Italian lines. Hundreds of thousands of Italian soldiers surrendered or deserted in panic following this surprise attack. Eleven thousand were killed, and twenty thousand were wounded. Frederic Henry is caught up in the chaotic retreat of soldiers and peasants.

The historic retreat took place in October 1917, before Hemingway went to Italy. To describe it, he drew on his memories of refugees marching in Turkey:

> In the column there were carts loaded with household goods; there were mirrors projecting up between mattresses, and chickens and ducks tied to carts. There was a sewing machine on the cart ahead of us in the rain. . . . On some carts the women sat huddled from the rain and others walked beside the carts keeping as close to them as they could. There were dogs now in the column, keeping under the wagons as they moved along.

Terrified Italian soldiers abandon their guns at Caporetto
in this illustration by the Hungarian artist Theo Matejko.

Upon reaching the Tagliamento River, the retreat bogs down. Frederic looks ahead and sees that the Italian police, needing scapegoats, are pulling military officers from the line and shooting them as deserters. Deciding to avoid this senseless fate, he jumps into the river. As Frederic swims to safety, *A Farewell to Arms* becomes an antiwar novel. Frederic's escape can be viewed symbolically, as the washing away of ideals formed in innocence. "I was always embarrassed by the words sacred, glorious, and sacrifice and the expression in vain," he says. "I had seen nothing sacred, and the things that were glorious had no glory and the sacrifices were like the stockyards of Chicago." Frederic finds Catherine, and together they go to Switzerland to await the birth of their child.

Here Hemingway paused to consider how his novel would end.

Should the baby live or die? He went back and forth, writing the ending first one way and then the other. He tried thirty-two endings before settling on one that satisfied him, one in which death wins. The baby is stillborn, and Catherine dies from complications of childbirth. Frederic loses everything: his regiment, his ideals, his child, and the woman he loves. At the novel's end, he leaves the hospital and returns to his hotel in the rain.

As soon as he read *A Farewell to Arms,* Maxwell Perkins knew that Hemingway had written a profound and important book. There was just one problem, in his opinion: the profanity. To make his conversations among fighting men sound authentic, Hemingway had included the strong language that real soldiers used in the war. Perkins pointed out that these words might hurt sales and cause the book to be banned in

Editor Maxwell Perkins deleted strong language from *A Farewell to Arms* against Hemingway's wishes. Still, throughout their long working relationship, the two men were close friends who went fishing together.

strait-laced cities such as Boston. Furthermore, *Scribner's Magazine* planned to print *A Farewell to Arms* in serial form. Such language could never appear in a publication that families kept on their coffee tables. Perkins therefore deleted "certain words" from the manuscript.

When Hemingway found out, he blew his top. "If a word can be printed and is needed in the text it is a *weakening* to omit it," he argued. He accused Perkins of halting the progress of literature. He predicted—correctly—that within a year other books would be published in the United States that contained the offending terms. Perkins gave in a little and put back words like bedpan and whore, which were unlikely to offend anyone, but he refused to allow the saltier language.

Even with the cuts, readers loved *A Farewell to Arms*. A literary critic for the *Chicago Tribune* saw in it the "blossoming of a most unusual genius of our day." She continued, "It is brutal, it is terrific, it is awesome, it is coarse, it is vulgar, it is beautiful, it is all sorts of contradictory things. But none of them counts, really, in comparison with the way that Mr. Hemingway has made it all of those things." A reviewer for the *New York Herald Tribune* concluded, "If anything better has been produced by a native of the New World I do not know what it is. And as for me, I have never gotten a greater kick out of any book."

A Farewell to Arms became a bestseller, even though in 1929 the Great Depression had started to spread its shadow of economic hardship over the world. For the next decade, millions of people endured unemployment, the loss of savings, hunger, and fear. Reading offered an escape, so for those who could spare a few dollars, buying a good book made sense. Thanks to steady sales, Hemingway weathered the depression in comfort. He also received $24,000 from a Hollywood studio that was making a movie of *A Farewell to Arms*.

With help from Uncle Gus Pfeiffer, he and Pauline bought an old square stone house at 907 Whitehead Street in Key West. The roof leaked, but lacy wrought-iron balconies adorned three of the sides. Palm and banyan trees graced the garden, where Ernest and Pauline kept unusual pets, including peacocks, raccoons, and an opossum.

Hemingway's enthusiasm for fishing and hunting was at its peak.

From Florida, he embarked with his male friends on fishing expeditions to the Dry Tortugas and the Marquesas Keys, islands known for their outstanding sportfishing. At times, these outings turned into great adventures. On a calm day in January 1930, Ernest, Max Perkins, the artist Mike Strater, and others took a rented boat to the Marquesas Keys, where Perkins caught a fifty-eight-pound kingfish with a rod and reel, breaking a world record. Suddenly, the sky and sea turned threatening. Dark clouds rolled in, the wind picked up, and the water rose in swells. A storm was coming on fast. As the waves grew to a horrific size, the fishermen took shelter in an old shed on a pier in the Tortugas. They had no way to let their families know they were safe, and as hours turned into days, their supply of food dwindled. They dropped fishing lines between the boards of the pier to catch their meals, and Ernest insisted that he never ate better. The men waited seventeen days for conditions to improve before returning to Key West, 77 miles away.

News of their return released their wives from the claws of dread. All had foreseen the worst—all except Pauline. She always counted on

Gary Cooper (left) starred in the 1932 Hollywood film based on Hemingway's novel *A Farewell to Arms.*

The Hemingway home in Key West as it appears today. Ernest wrote in the upstairs room of the carriage house.

Today, Hemingway's writing studio looks much as it did when he worked there. In this room, he created some of his best-known novels, short stories, and nonfiction books.

Ernest's ability to survive in tough situations and had never doubted his safety. He admired this trait in his wife.

Ernest hunted during family vacations on the L Bar T ranch in Wyoming, which was owned by a couple named Olive and Lawrence Nordquist. In the wooded mountain country, he went after bear, elk, and other large game. In August 1930, in response to complaints from neighboring ranchers that a bear was killing their cattle, Ernest and one of the ranch hands shot a horse and left its carcass in the woods as bait. Several days later, when they returned to the spot and saw a bear feeding on the dead horse, Ernest killed it with a single shot. He spent the next three days fishing and caught ninety-two trout. On August 30, when he took Bumby to see the dead horse, another bear had come to feed. Again, Ernest killed it with his first shot.

In September, with summer over, Pauline left for New York with Bumby, who was sailing home to France. Ernest stayed on in Wyoming, and on October 21, John Dos Passos arrived for ten days of hunting, although he was too nearsighted to be a good shot. The camaraderie that Hemingway enjoyed with the ranch hands impressed his friend from the

East. "They thought he was the most wonderful guy they had ever met," Dos Passos said.

When the time for hunting was over and Hemingway and Dos Passos prepared for the long drive to Key West, a ranch hand named Floyd Allington asked to come along. An avid fisherman, Allington was eager to go after the big fish that swam in the waters off Florida. After a night of camping in Yellowstone National Park, the three men headed toward Billings, Montana, where they would pick up the highway. The carefree adventure ended at dusk, when a car traveling in the opposite direction pulled into their lane and headed straight toward them. Hemingway was at the wheel and turned sharply to the right. He avoided a head-on collision, but his Ford rolled over in the ditch that ran alongside the road.

Hemingway poses with the skins of bears he killed while staying at the Nordquists' ranch in Wyoming.

Allington and Dos Passos escaped serious injury; Hemingway emerged from the overturned vehicle with a badly broken right arm. A passing motorist drove the three to St. Vincent's Hospital in Billings, where Ernest had surgery to set his bones. Pauline came as soon as she could and was amazed to see her husband endure so much pain with great courage. "I have never seen anyone behave so beautifully," she remarked.

For a month, Hemingway rested in bed without moving—doctor's orders. He talked with the patients across the hall, two farm workers who had been shot while drinking coffee in a restaurant late at night. He also befriended Sister Florence Cloonan, a Catholic nun who lived to nurse patients and talk about baseball. But unable to write and with little to do, he grew depressed. He continued his long, boring recovery in Piggott, where he, Pauline, and Patrick spent Christmas, and then in Key West.

The Hemingways also made trips to Europe, but for Ernest in these years, Europe meant Spain. In summer 1929, he had returned with Pauline to the festival in Pamplona and traveled throughout Spain, seeing bullfights. That summer he began a friendship with the matador Sidney Franklin, who had been born and raised in Brooklyn, New York. Franklin learned to fight bulls in Mexico and had recently entered Spanish bullrings for the first time. Hemingway admired Franklin's "cold, serene, and intelligent valor." Hoping to enjoy a friendship untouched by the aura of his fame, he passed himself off as an ordinary *aficionado* and said nothing about being a writer. Later, when someone told Franklin who Hemingway was, the matador found it hard to believe. Hemingway considered this a great compliment.

Ernest Hemingway had a great love of bullfighting and knew enough about it to fill a whole book. As the 1930s dawned, he decided to write that book. The writing was well under way by November 12, 1931, when Ernest and Pauline's second child was born. Ernest had hoped for a girl, but the baby was a nine-pound boy, whom they named Gregory.

Soon afterward, Ernest's new book entered the world. *Death in the Afternoon,* which was published in 1932, was a guide to modern Spanish bullfighting. In it Hemingway explained countless technical details of the sport, from the roles of the banderilleros, picadors, and matador to the

In *Death in the Afternoon,* Hemingway praised matador Sidney Franklin's style in the bullring.

breeding of bulls for the ring. He created word portraits of famous modern matadors, discussed the technique of killing with a sword, and defined hundreds of bullfighting terms.

He also digressed, just as he would in conversation with a friend. He described the aftermath of violence that he had witnessed in the war, and he revealed some of the lessons he had learned about crafting fiction. "When writing a novel a writer should create living people," he told his readers. "People in a novel, not skillfully constructed *characters,* must be projected from the writer's assimilated experience, from his knowledge, from his head, from his heart and from all there is of him." He delved into his theory of omission, the notion that a skilled writer can omit information yet allow it to influence a story. He compared these unwritten details and their force to the unseen mass of an iceberg, which has the power to sink ships.

In *Death in the Afternoon,* Hemingway explained why bullfighting repelled some spectators, including many Americans. To appreciate a bullfight, people had to be "fascinated by death, its nearness and its avoidance," he maintained. They also needed to appreciate the courage of the matador, to understand that "it takes more cojones to be a sportsman when death is a closer party to the game."

Cojones . . . manhood . . . courage. Hemingway thought often about what courage and cowardice meant. He defined courage as "grace under pressure," and compared a courageous person to a soldier who understood that "danger only exists at the moment of danger." This person had learned to turn off the imagination in a time of crisis and live completely in the present. He or she did what needed to be done without thinking of the worst that could happen. Hemingway understood that in any tough situation, "Whatever I had to do men had always done." He insisted, "If they had done it then I could do it too and the best thing was not to worry about it." Yet he needed to test himself.

Hunting dangerous game offered the tests of courage he sought. In 1932, he, Pauline, and their friend Charles Thompson journeyed to east Africa, home of the lion, elephant, rhino, and zebra, to go on a hunting safari. After reaching the Kenyan city of Mombasa, on the Indian Ocean, they traveled inland by rail for three hundred miles. Their train crossed arid grasslands before climbing to a broad, lofty plateau and stopping in Nairobi, the capital of Kenya. There, Hemingway and the others met their guide, Philip Percival. Hunters coming to Africa needed a guide to lead them to game and offer instruction that might save their lives. A guide pointed out the circling vultures that meant lions were on the savannah, feasting on their kill. A guide taught a hunter how to approach a wounded animal and be safe from mauling.

The gray-haired Percival had been born in England but had immigrated to British East Africa in 1905, at age twenty. He had served as a guide to other illustrious hunters, including Theodore Roosevelt and Winston Churchill. He owned a farm in the hill country southeast of Nairobi, where Hemingway and his party stayed while they shot gazelle, impala, and guinea fowl. Once their bodies adjusted to the region's greater elevation, they set out for the Serengeti, the great plain of Africa. Stretching from southwest Kenya to the northern section of modern Tanzania (then called Tanganyika), the region is home to seventy large-mammal species and more than five hundred kinds of birds. Enormous herds of wildebeest grazed on the savannah, just as bison once covered the American prairie. Snowcapped Mount Kilimanjaro ruled the horizon like an exalted African king. Hemingway had never seen such a beautiful place, and in 1933, the quantity of African game seemed limitless.

The hunters rode in high, open vehicles, while two trucks carried their tents and camping gear. The caravan covered two hundred miles before making camp beside a stream. Over the next ten days, the Hemingways and Thompson killed two leopards and many eland, antelope, and gazelle, collecting antlers and skins to bring home as souvenirs and gifts.

Around the campfire at night, Percival entertained the others with stories of his long years in the bush. He spoke of hunters who had overcome cowardice in a moment of danger, and he described the strangeness of the natural world. He told one tale about a climber who discovered the frozen body of a leopard near the snowy top of Mount Kilimanjaro, far beyond the animal's usual range.

The safari had barely begun when Ernest came down with amoebic dysentery, an intestinal illness caused by microorganisms found in contaminated food or water. He mustered up his strength and stayed with the hunt despite having a fever, stomach pains, and severe diarrhea. He followed game in a car or truck rather than on foot, and if he felt dizzy, he leaned against a tree to shoot. He managed to kill two lions in this weakened state, but his condition worsened. In mid-January, he felt great pain as part of his intestine prolapsed, or moved out of its proper position in the body. Percival insisted that he seek treatment and arranged by two-way radio for him to be flown to Nairobi.

Bed rest and injections of emetrine, a drug that kills amoebas, restored Ernest's health. On January 23, he rejoined Pauline and the others on safari, just in time to move into hilly country and hunt rhinoceros, sable, and kudu. "This was the kind of hunting I liked," he said. It gladdened him to walk and shoot freely at whatever game he encountered, "to

Four hunters in Africa show off trophies of the horned animals they shot. From left to right are Philip Percival's assistant, Ben Fourie; Charles Thompson; Percival; and Hemingway.

feel the grass under my soft-soled shoes and the pleasant weight of the rifle, held just back of the muzzle, the barrel resting on my shoulder, and the sun hot enough to sweat you well as it burned the dew from the grass." He noted, "I had been quite ill and had the pleasant feeling of getting stronger each day."

Hemingway enjoyed the simple sensations of hunting, but he could not help wanting to shoot the biggest and the best. The hunt became a competition for him, and Charles Thompson was winning. On the day Hemingway felled a rhinoceros from a stunning distance of three hundred yards, Thompson shot a larger one with a longer horn. Thompson's lion was bigger, and so were his leopard and buffalo. Hemingway felt elated when he killed two bull kudu, antelopes prized for their long, spiraled horns. Then he saw Thompson's final trophy, "the biggest, widest, darkest, longest-curling, heaviest, most unbelievable pair of kudu horns" he had ever seen.

Percival reminded Hemingway that humans "have very primitive emotions," and that it is "impossible not to be competitive." Jealousy and the drive to compete can be destructive, however, and need to be controlled. With effort, Hemingway got over his disappointment and took pleasure in his friend's success as well as his own. He left Africa feeling "hungry for more of it," and promised himself that he would return soon.

While he was on safari, his next collection of stories, *Winner Take Nothing,* was published. This book contained some of Hemingway's finest short stories, including "A Way You'll Never Be," in which Nick Adams is shot in the knee while fighting for the Italians in the war. Nick also is wounded psychologically by the terrible things he has seen, and again Hemingway described the swollen, unburied bodies he saw in Italy after the war, which still troubled his mind.

In another outstanding story, "A Clean, Well-Lighted Place," Hemingway gives refuge to a character who is tempted by suicide, something he was never able to do for his father. In a café like the ones where Hemingway drank in Spain, two waiters discuss a customer, an old, deaf man who lingers and sips brandy in the hours after midnight. Recently, the old man tried to kill himself. The younger waiter is eager to close up and go home to his family, but his coworker is patient with the old customer. For him as well, nothingness lurks like a predator just beyond the clean, bright atmosphere of the café. "It was a nothing that he knew too well," Hemingway wrote. "Some lived in it and never felt it but he knew it all was *nada y pues nada y nada y pues nada* [nothing and therefore nothing and nothing and therefore nothing]."

Other stories in the book fell short of the standard of excellence that Hemingway had set in his best work. They lacked the emotional power that his readers admired. Also, many people had tired of his favorite subjects: war, brutality, and bullfighting. "I can't feel that your stories about sport and sudden death lead to anything large or profound," wrote book reviewer Clifton Fadiman in an open letter to Hemingway. "As literary material, you have developed these things to the saturation point. Why not go on with something else?"

With the safari at its end, the "something else" that most attracted Hemingway was fishing. As soon as his ship docked in Manhattan, he went straight to a shipyard in neighboring Brooklyn to order a thirty-eight-foot diesel-powered cabin cruiser. It was a big, sturdy boat for deep-sea fishing, painted black and green. Hemingway would wait thirty days for his new boat to be delivered to Florida, but he had already chosen its name: the *Pilar*.

NINE

"Wonderful...Irreplaceable...Impossible"

Ernest Hemingway had become a Key West tourist attraction. Vacationers peered through the fence around his house or waved to him as he piloted the *Pilar* into open water. Island visitors looked for him in Sloppy Joe's, where rum had been served legally since December 5, 1933, when a Constitutional amendment repealed Prohibition. His circle of drinking buddies had grown to include World War I veterans employed by the Civilian Conservation Corps (CCC), a government agency that gave work to young men during the depression. These CCC workers were building the Overseas Highway, connecting the Florida Keys to the mainland.

In his everyday uniform of bare feet, stained white trousers, and a jaunty captain's cap, Hemingway sailed to Cuba and the Bahamas. On the narrow island of Bimini, he discovered beautiful beaches almost untouched by tourism, where sparkling turquoise water washed against the shore and deepened into the solid blue of the Gulf Stream. He imagined being "at the end of the world."

Pauline loved the island, too. She and the children stayed there on land while Ernest fished for marlin, kingfish, and tuna. "Go wherever you

The captain of
the *Pilar* waves to
friends on shore.

want, kids. There's plenty of Bimini to explore and you can't get lost
here," he told his boys.

Hemingway was seldom alone on his fishing trips. New friends and
old were often onboard the *Pilar*. Among the frequent guests were two
ichthyologists from Philadelphia who were reclassifying the various
species of marlin; a wealthy American couple named Jane and Grant
Mason; and a Cuban painter, Antonio Gattorno. Gattorno observed that
Hemingway's mood shifted between gloom and euphoria, and that he
consumed alcohol from morning until night. His symptoms and behavior
match the condition that used to be called manic depression but today is
known as bipolar disorder.

Modern readers can often only speculate about the health problems
of famous people from the past, even with accounts like Gattorno's as evidence. It is hard to know, for example, if Gattorno was an unbiased witness or if he had many opportunities to observe his host. In contrast, the
unusual number of Hemingways who took their own lives clearly demon-

strates that suicidal depression ran in the family. It afflicted Ed Hemingway, at least three of his children (Ernest, Ursula, and Leicester), and Ernest's granddaughter Margaux Hemingway.

Papa's old friends also noticed troubling signs that he was losing control. He was behaving recklessly, carrying on an affair with the beautiful and unstable Jane Mason, and attacking sea creatures as though they were enemies. On an April 1935 fishing trip with John Dos Passos and Mike Strater, Hemingway hooked a large shark. He reeled the fish to the side of the boat, but before lifting it on deck, he pulled out a pistol to shoot it in the head. At that moment, the gaff holding the fish slipped. Ernest accidentally shot himself in both legs and had to be rushed ashore for treatment. The wounds were painful but superficial, and after a week of rest, he was back in his boat.

After sharks devoured a tuna he had just caught on another outing, he bought a Thompson submachine gun— a Tommy gun—and vowed to defend his catch in the future. He saw a chance to use it near Bimini, when sharks approached a marlin that Strater was reeling in. Strater begged him not to shoot, but he fired at the sharks anyway; blood flowed into the surrounding water and attracted more sharks, which led to a feeding frenzy. Very little of the marlin was left when an angry Strater hoisted it into the boat.

Hemingway was "fed up with the world, and I was fed up with him," said the poet Archibald MacLeish, another fellow fisherman. "He was a wonderful, an irreplaceable but an impossible friend."

John and Katy Dos Passos thought Hemingway's fame had gone to his

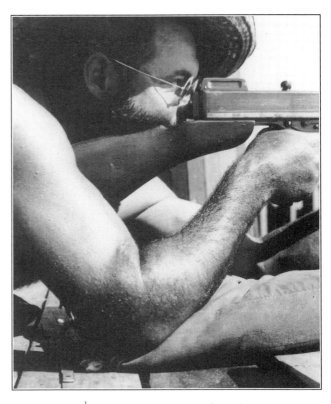

Hemingway practices firing his Tommy gun.

head. To them, he was trying to live up to his reputation as the "famous author, the great sports fisherman, the mighty African hunter." John Dos Passos said, "We tried to keep him kidded down to size." Darker issues troubled their friend, however. A month earlier, Hemingway had written to a couple who lost their son, "I know that anyone who dies young after a happy childhood . . . has won a great victory. We all have to look forward to death by defeat, our bodies gone, our world destroyed; but it is the same dying we must do, while he has gotten it all over with." The man who wrote these glum, weary words was only thirty-five years old.

Between fishing trips, Hemingway wrote. He completed a book about Africa that was intended to be a true account of his safari adventure, written in the style of a novel. It was an experiment, an attempt "to write an absolutely true book to see whether the shape of the country and the pattern of a month's action can, if truly presented, compete with a work of the imagination." He challenged himself to stick to the facts while offering vivid descriptions, fully developed characters, and a well-paced narrative. Just as he would in a novel, he created dialogue and moved inside characters' heads to reveal their thoughts. He finished the book thinking it might be the best thing he had ever written and called it *Green Hills of Africa*.

Hemingway's travels had taken him as far as the east coast of Africa and the American West. He had felt the horror of war and—to his way of thinking—matched himself against some of the world's strongest and most dangerous creatures. He had yet to experience the full, furious power of nature, but he did so on Labor Day weekend in 1935, when a

One of the approximately sixty cats at the Hemingway home in Key West shows off its extra toes. The polydactyl cats living on the property today are said to be descendants of a six-toed feline that was given to Hemingway by a sea captain in 1935. Gregory Hemingway called this story false, pointing out that his mother never would have allowed her peacocks to be chased by cats. Regardless of their ancestry, the animals are popular with the many tourists who visit the Ernest Hemingway Home and Museum.

Hemingway enjoys a day of fishing in Key West.

monstrous hurricane struck the Keys. Knowing a storm was on the way, Hemingway boarded up his windows and carried outdoor toys and lawn furniture inside. He secured the *Pilar* in the island's submarine basin and went home to wait out the rough weather. At midnight, with killer winds tearing down trees, he made his way on foot to the submarine basin to be sure his boat was safe. He stood guard, lashed by wind and rain, with terrific lightning flashing overhead, until five A.M., when the gale began to lessen.

The hurricane damaged many of the buildings and gardens of Key West. To the east, on Windley, Long, and Lower Matecumbe keys, it proved deadly. Winds moving at two hundred miles per hour destroyed

The commissioners and school board of Monroe County, Florida, erected this monument to the victims of the hurricane of September 2, 1935.

houses, and a storm tide of eighteen feet washed railroad cars out to sea. The wind lifted a beam of wood eighteen feet long and sent it crashing through a cabin three hundred feet away. It peeled railroad tracks and crossties from a concrete viaduct rising thirty feet above the normal water level. More than five hundred people died, many of them veterans working for the CCC. Hemingway blamed the bureaucrats in Washington, D.C., for the veterans' deaths. A train had been readied to carry them to safe ground as soon as the storm was predicted, but government officials held it up, believing the men were in no danger and evacuation was a waste of money. When the train eventually was sent in, it was too late. The surging water knocked it off the tracks.

With the sea still choppy, Hemingway hired his friend Bra Saunders, an experienced sailor, to take him to see the worst devastation. Along shorelines that had been stripped of vegetation and violently reshaped overnight, he saw "more dead than I'd seen in one place since the lower Piave in June 1918." He saw bodies floating in the water, entangled in branches, or partially buried in the sand.

He was still feeling the distress brought on by these shocking sights when his emotions received a second blow: disappointing reviews for *Green Hills of Africa*. "It used to be pretty exciting, sitting down to read a new book by Hemingway, but now it's damn near alarming," wrote one critic. "He thinks he can write a piece about anything and get away with it." Another proclaimed it "not exactly a poor book, but it is certainly far from a good one." Edmund Wilson, who had championed Hemingway's first books, thought he was at his weakest when writing about himself.

Hemingway "is certainly his own worst-drawn character, and he is his own worst commentator. His very prose style goes to pot," Wilson declared.

Someone needing to be the biggest and the best found comments like these hard to take. Hemingway fell into a funk. He confided to Pauline's mother that he had come to understand the torments that depressed people suffer. "It makes me more tolerant of what happened to my father," he said. He might make such a statement privately, but never in print for the public to read, as his old friend F. Scott Fitzgerald did. Between February and April 1936, Fitzgerald published three essays in *Esquire* magazine describing his own mental breakdown. These were included in his 1945 book *The Crack-Up*.

Yet during this rough emotional spell, Hemingway produced two short-story masterworks. He was thinking of Philip Percival's tale of the leopard frozen to death when he wrote "The Snows of Kilimanjaro." This story centers on a writer named Harry who is dying of gangrene. Harry and his wife are stranded on the African grassland because their truck has broken down. As they wait for another vehicle to come or for a plane that will fly Harry to a hospital, vultures and hyenas, the local scavengers, bide their time. Like Harry, they sense the approach of death. While waiting, Harry thinks about past events that he had planned to write about one day and regrets that he has run out of time.

Hemingway employed the stream-of-consciousness technique to present the flow of memories through Harry's mind. Recalling a week spent snowbound in Austria, when he played cards by lantern light, causes Harry to remember a snowy Christmas during the Great War, when an Allied machine gunner mowed down Austrian officers escaping a train that had been bombed. Similarly, thoughts of fleeing bitter arguments with his first wife by taking a lonely trip to Constantinople bring to mind a night in Paris when he thought he spotted her on a boulevard. *"He had seen the world change,"* Hemingway wrote. *"He had been in it and he had watched it and it was his duty to write of it; but now he never would."*

The dying Harry dreams that a plane comes to rescue him. It carries him into the sky, but instead of heading toward the town of Arusha to refuel, the pilot flies in the opposite direction. The dying man sees "as wide as all the world, great, high, and unbelievably white in the sun . . . the square top of Kilimanjaro."

At one point in the story, Harry thinks about F. Scott Fitzgerald as a washed-up writer, one who thought of the rich as "a special glamourous race and when he found they weren't it wrecked him just as much as any other thing that wrecked him." Hemingway used the story to distance himself from Fitzgerald's mental weakness, but these lines brought him a scolding letter from his old pal. Fitzgerald may have written about profound, personal issues, but "it doesn't mean I want friends praying aloud over my corpse," he noted. Hemingway fired off an insulting reply, leading Fitzgerald to observe that old Hem was "quite as nervously broken down as I am but it manifests itself in different ways." ("The Snows of Kilimanjaro" has been reprinted many times with the name Julian substituted for Fitzgerald.)

The second story, "The Short Happy Life of Francis Macomber," also features an American couple hunting in Africa. Macomber and his wife, Margot, are locked in a loveless marriage that neither can bear to leave. "He was very wealthy, and would be much wealthier, and he knew she would not leave him ever now," the narrator explains. "His wife had been a great beauty and she was still a great beauty in Africa, but she was not a great enough beauty anymore at home to be able to leave him and better herself and she knew it and he knew it."

The story opens after a morning lion hunt in which Francis ran from the wounded, charging beast in a great show of cowardice. Margot takes pleasure in humiliating him further. During the next day's buffalo hunt, however, Francis summons courage he did not know he possessed and holds his ground against three mature bulls. He feels elated, but Margot appears ashen and afraid. The balance of power in the marriage has changed, and her position is no longer secure.

Francis and the guide, Robert Wilson, thought they killed all three buffalo, but one is only wounded. As Margot waits in the car, the two men go after the third bull to complete the kill. Suddenly, the wounded buffalo rushes toward them, and Francis shoots. Then "he felt a sudden white-hot, blinding flash explode inside his head and that was all he ever felt." Margot has shot him from the car but insists that she aimed for the buffalo. The story's complexity stems largely from this act. Did Margot murder her husband, as Wilson believes? Did she aim for him unconsciously, or was the shooting accidental?

In July 1936, Hemingway's attention turned from Africa to Spain, where civil war was threatening people's freedom. Spain's political situation had been unstable since April 1931, when King Alfonso XIII fled Madrid to live in exile in Rome. For the first time, Spain was a republic with an elected president. But after the left-leaning Popular Front won the February 1936 election with less than a majority of votes, the country fell into chaos. Church burnings, political assassinations, and strikes occurred nearly every day. Two powerful labor unions battled each other with guns. When General Francisco Franco led a military uprising on July 17, he had support from the millions of Spaniards who had voted for the rightist National Front. His Nationalists also had help from Fascist Italy and Nazi Germany.

Franco's followers declared him chief of the Spanish state on October 1, but Spaniards loyal to the republican government (the Loyalists or Republicans) fought to bring him down. Sympathetic volunteers from the

Young Germans, many of them wearing uniforms of the Hitler Youth, visit San Sebastian, in Nationalist-held Spain. Nazi Germany supported General Francisco Franco's forces in the Spanish Civil War.

United States and other countries were taking up arms alongside the Loyalists, forming military units known as the International Brigades. Many were intellectuals or writers who admired the Soviet Union, which was backing the Republican cause. Hemingway had no love for communism, but he hated war and fascism, and he believed in the rightness of a freely elected government. He donated two ambulances to the Loyalist cause, but he wanted to do more.

That fall, when John Wheeler, director of the North American Newspaper Alliance (NANA), asked him to go to Spain and report on the war for newspapers throughout the United States, Hemingway jumped at the chance. He would be able to see for himself what was happening in a land that was close to his heart, gain new material for his writing, and feel excitement and freedom once again. To Hemingway, being a married man with children felt more and more like living in a cage, and his relationship with Pauline was breaking down.

Wheeler's offer came as Hemingway was finishing a novel called *To Have and Have Not*. In this book, Hemingway's only novel set in the United States, he contrasts the lives of Americans struggling through the Great Depression with those of the wealthy. The rich "haves" whom he portrays, a collection of writers, artists, and socialites, are sad, dishonest, and disillusioned. The main character, Harry Morgan, represents the "have nots." Morgan earns a living by chartering his fishing boat and smuggling goods and people from Cuba into Key West. He embodies qualities Hemingway admires: He fishes, he fights, he can hold his liquor, and he is brave. Morgan barely flinches when a bullet shatters his arm and it later must be amputated.

Morgan has trouble finding the right words and speaking fluently. Nevertheless he expresses the theme that lies at the core of Hemingway's third novel, that human beings all face challenges and need one another's support. "One man alone ain't got. No man alone now," Harry says. "No matter how a man alone ain't got no bloody fucking chance." This sounded like a new view of life from the author who fought his way through tough times relying on his own courage and physical strength. It sounded to many people as though Hemingway was developing a social conscience. (With the publication of *To Have and Have Not,* Hemingway would achieve the freedom of language he had long sought.)

Hemingway was relaxing at Sloppy Joe's one night in December 1936 when in walked twenty-eight-year-old Martha Gellhorn of St. Louis, who was vacationing in Florida with her mother and younger brother. Gellhorn was a journalist who had published a novel and a book of short stories. She corresponded with First Lady Eleanor Roosevelt, and she had lived in Europe. She also hated fascism and was eager to report on the war in Spain. Ernest liked this smart, sophisticated, tall young woman. He showed her around Key West and introduced her to Pauline. Martha's stay stretched into January 1937, lasting weeks after her mother and brother had gone home.

Ernest desired more than friendship, though. He took a business trip to New York when Martha was returning to St. Louis. He met her in Miami for dinner and then rode with her on a northbound train until their routes diverged. From St. Louis Martha wrote to Pauline as though she were a friend, "You are a fine girl and it was good of you not to mind my becoming a fixture, like a kudu head, in your home."

Before leaving for Spain, Hemingway arranged with John Dos Passos, playwright Lillian Hellman, and Dutch filmmaker Joris Ivens to make a documentary that would be used to raise money for the Republican cause. Hemingway agreed to write the film's narration. He reached Spain in March 1937 and moved into the Hotel Florida in Madrid, where the sound of gunfire could be heard all night long. He was soon joined by Dos Passos, matador

Hemingway felt a strong attraction to smart, ambitious Martha Gellhorn.

When in the field with Spanish Republican soldiers, Hemingway lived as they did, even if that meant eating from a can.

Sidney Franklin, and Gellhorn, who was covering the war for *Collier's Magazine.*

The city remained a Republican stronghold, but the enemy bombarded it from without. Parents kept their children indoors. With supplies scarce, people stood in line all day to buy food. If Fascist shelling forced them to scatter, then their families went hungry. The government urged civilians to leave Madrid, but most stayed on. "Why do they stay?" Hemingway asked. "They stay because this is their city, these are their homes, here is their work, this is their fight."

He and Gellhorn traveled to the front, often with filmmaker Ivens. "Hemingway liked to accompany me," Ivens said, "because my direct connections with the General Staff of the Republican Army and the International Brigades enabled me to get much closer to the front lines than other correspondents could. We became good friends. Because he was strong he carried the movie camera." At times, Hemingway and the film crew got so close to the action that they had to run from incoming artillery fire. In the field, Hemingway munched on raw onions that he pulled from his pockets and drank whiskey from a silver flask. He shared his liquor with the filmmakers, but they said no thank you to the onions.

In both his film script and his news stories for NANA, Hemingway focused on the Republican side of the war, never trying to be an unbiased reporter. He described a woman old enough to be a grandmother bleeding from a chest wound, shot by the Nationalists; streets covered with shattered glass and pulverized brick and smelling of smoke; an exploding artillery shell sending up a spray of black Spanish soil; and men who had been stonemasons and lawyers fighting for their country. In villages he saw boys being drilled in military tactics. He carefully noticed how the freedom fighters dressed and behaved; he listened closely when they spoke to one another.

At times, Hemingway did more than simply observe. He showed a soldier how to stop his rifle from jamming by hitting the bolt with a rock. He even picked up a gun and fought for the side he thought was in the right. Exposed to gunfire and shelling, he had many chances to demonstrate grace under pressure. He also saved the life of *New York Times* reporter Herbert Matthews—as well as his own—when the two men were crossing the Ebro River by boat. The current was strong, so someone on the far shore pulled the boat with a rope. Suddenly, the line broke, and the boat headed downstream toward dangerous rapids. Showing unusual strength, Hemingway grabbed the oars and rowed the boat across. Matthews called him "a good man in a pinch."

Hemingway left Spain in May to show Ivens's film, *The Spanish Earth*, in New York City and Los Angeles. He had not yet recorded the narration when the film was shown for the first time, on June 4, at Carnegie Hall in New York, so the audience watched in silence as images moved across the screen. Hemingway almost never gave speeches and nervously pulled at his tie as he stepped before the crowd. But as he stated his reasons for being in Spain, he forgot his jitters and spoke easily and powerfully. "There is only one form of government that cannot produce good writers, and that system is fascism," he said. "For fascism is a lie told by bullies. A writer who will not lie cannot live under fascism."

"The Totalitarian fascist states believe in the Totalitarian war," he said. That simply meant, he explained, "that whenever they are beaten by armed forces they take their revenge on unarmed civilians." In this war, "Every time they are beaten in the field they salvage that strange thing they call their honor, by murdering civilians."

He defended his own honor in August, when he ran into his old friend Max Eastman while visiting Maxwell Perkins at his office. Hemingway remembered Eastman from the international conference in Genoa that they both had covered in 1922. In 1933, Eastman had written an unkind review of *Death in the Afternoon*. He had accused Hemingway of displaying "an enthusiasm for killing" and writing as though he wore "false hair on the chest."

Face-to-face with the author of this review, Hemingway unbuttoned his shirt to prove that his chest hair was real. He then pulled open Eastman's to reveal smooth, hairless skin. Eastman was about to explain his words when Hemingway pushed an open book in his face, and the two men tussled on the floor. Hemingway later told reporters that Eastman had "jumped at me like a woman, clawing. . . . I just held him off. I didn't want to hurt him."

Stopping in at home, he played war games on the lawn with Patrick and Gregory. "He had brought back firecrackers, so we had imaginary armies moving into battle against each other, complete with cannon fire and puffs of smoke," Gregory Hemingway recalled as an adult. "God, how I wanted to go back to Spain with him when he left."

Hemingway persuaded people to donate thousands of dollars for the Loyalist cause before he returned to Madrid in the fall. In all, he made four trips to Spain in 1937 and 1938, with Martha Gellhorn as his close companion. While in Madrid he started to write a play inspired by his experiences during the war, with characters based on himself and Gellhorn. It was the only work for the stage he would ever write. He called it *The*

Hemingway's three boys: Patrick, Bumby, and Gregory.

Fifth Column, which was the name given to Nationalist agents in Madrid who were seeking to undermine the Republican government. The term now refers to any group working secretly to bring down a larger group or nation while appearing to be loyal. Hemingway's play ends on a bitter note, reflecting his awareness that the Loyalists controlled an ever-shrinking portion of the country and were losing the war. It came as no surprise to him to learn that on March 28, 1939, Nationalist forces entered Madrid; on April 1, Franco announced that the Republican army had surrendered.

Hemingway doubted that a lasting peace had been achieved. As early as 1935, he predicted that another major war would soon erupt in Europe. "France is a country and Great Britain is several countries but Italy is a man, Mussolini, and Germany is a man, Hitler," he had written then. "A man has ambitions, a man rules until he gets into economic trouble; he tries to get out of this trouble by war."

TEN

Life Is Now

"A stupid and foolish book, a disgrace to a good writer, a book which never should have been printed . . ."

A novel displaying "shocking lapses from professional skill . . ."

Most critics dismissed *To Have and Have Not* with comments like these. Readers had waited eight years for a new novel by Ernest Hemingway, and this one disappointed them. People shook their heads and said that the most famous author in the world was faltering. Whether the remaining pages of Hemingway's life "are to reach a further climax, are to be torn off unfinished or peter out in a dull decline, time alone can tell," concluded the writers of *Time* magazine. Hemingway grumbled that the critics were ganging up on him.

In truth, though, he was living through a rough chapter in the story of his life. He knew his recent work lacked the brilliance of his earlier stories and novels, and this terrified him. His marriage to Pauline was over, and she had reacted to the breakup with deep sadness that turned into anger. Still feeling that he could confide in Hadley, Ernest admitted to her, "Life is quite complicated." He was doing his best to stay strong and "not get discouraged and take the easy way out," as his father had done. Suicide would set a "very bad example to the children," he believed.

After leaving Spain, Ernest went to live in Cuba with Martha. They rented a rundown farmhouse on fifteen acres, a place called Finca Vigía (Lookout Farm). As Martha took charge of repairing the Spanish-style house and cleaning up the grounds, Ernest wrote, Cuba's gentle ocean breezes calmed his heart and helped the words flow easily once more. Again, he was in top form, writing as only he knew how to do. On March 1, 1939, with Spain's Republican government about to collapse, he started a novel inspired by everything he had seen and done in the Spanish Civil War. He wrote steadily, even when the living-room ceiling crashed to the floor, covering everything with powdered plaster. He wrote as rain came in, turning the plaster into a hard, white crust.

Recalling the old European custom of announcing a death with the

Open windows let in warm Cuban breezes while Hemingway writes.

ringing of church bells, he titled this novel *For Whom the Bell Tolls*. The words themselves came from "Meditation XVII," an essay by the seventeenth-century English poet and writer John Donne. "Any man's death diminishes me because I am involved in mankind," Donne had written; "therefore never send to know for whom the bell tolls; it tolls for thee."

It was a fitting title, because awareness that death is ever near causes Hemingway's main character, Robert Jordan, to live fully in the present during the roughly three days of the novel's action. "I suppose it is possible to live as full a life in seventy hours as in seventy years," Jordan thinks. "And if there is not any such thing as a long time . . . but there is only now, why then now is the thing to praise and I am very happy with it."

Robert has good reason to think he may not have much time left. A college professor from Montana, he has volunteered to aid the Loyalist side in the Spanish Civil War. Because he knows how to use explosives, he is ordered to blow up a bridge. Assisting him in this dangerous mission is a band of civilians-turned-guerilla-fighters who have taken refuge in a mountain cave. Hemingway based these characters on the fighting men and women he had met in the Spanish countryside. The leader of this fictional band, a man named Pablo, adheres to the "principle of the fox": If he avoids making a disturbance, then the enemy is less likely to hunt him out of the mountains. Once fearless, Pablo now cares more about staying alive than aiding the cause. Robert suspects he may sabotage the mission.

Robert detects true courage in Pablo's wife, Pilar. This sturdy, sharp-tongued woman has witnessed atrocities and helped blow up a train. She has been caring for Maria, a younger woman who was the victim of Fascist violence. Early in the war, Franco's soldiers murdered Maria's parents and the mayor of her town. They repeatedly raped her and then forced her into the local barbershop and cut off all her hair. In this time of war, when death can come at any moment, Maria and Robert quickly fall in love. They talk about the future, but Robert understands they have none. Because of the war, they will have "Not time, not happiness, not

Hemingway based the Loyalist guerillas in *For Whom the Bell Tolls* on real Spanish fighting men like these. He brought this photograph home from Spain and kept it for the rest of his life.

fun, not children, not a house, not a bathroom, not a clean pair of pyjamas, not the morning paper, not to wake up together, not to wake and know she's there and that you're not alone." He tells himself that he has love at this moment, "and that is all your whole life is: now. There is nothing else than now."

Pablo runs off with some of the explosives from Robert's pack, hoping to halt the mission. He has a change of heart and returns with additional men, but he has thrown away the stolen detonator caps. Robert and the others move on to the bridge, and they succeed in blowing it up with the dynamite that is left. Then, fleeing on horseback, they must cross a road that is protected by a Nationalist tank and expose themselves to enemy fire. An exploding shell causes Robert's horse to fall on him, and his left leg is broken. To carry a badly injured comrade would slow the escape and jeopardize the group's safety; Robert knows he has reached the end. He tells Maria that she must live for him as well. "Thou art me too now. Thou art all there will be of me."

Maria and the others leave him behind with a machine gun. Alone, Robert reflects on his brief but full life: "You've had just as good a life as grandfather's though not as long. You've had as good a life as any one because of these last days." He considers killing himself to avoid capture and the torture that is bound to follow, but he rejects suicide. He instead plans to shoot at the Fascists, hoping to kill at least one before they open fire on him and end his pain. In this way he may give the survivors a little more time to escape.

Hemingway dedicated his novel to Martha Gellhorn, whom he married in November 1940. "Anyhow, it is a hell of a book," he informed Max Perkins. When *For Whom the Bell Tolls* was published, most people agreed. Ernest Hemingway had written something "rare and beautiful," gushed the critic for the *Atlantic Monthly* in a typical review. "He has done his finest work, and, what is perhaps more important, he has dispelled any fears concerning his own limitations."

Relieved that he had redeemed himself, Ernest sent an autographed copy of his book to F. Scott Fitzgerald, who responded with honest praise. "It's a fine novel, better than anyone else writing could do," Fitzgerald wrote. He promised "to read the whole thing again," but he never had the chance. Six weeks later, the forty-four-year-old novelist died of a heart attack in Hollywood, California.

For Whom the Bell Tolls made its author a wealthy man. Readers bought almost a half million copies of the novel in six months, and Paramount Pictures paid him a hundred thousand dollars for the film rights. Hemingway purchased Finca Vigía and adopted a celebrity's lifestyle. In the 1940s, he vacationed in Sun Valley, Idaho, a resort community in the foothills of the Rocky Mountains that offered hunting, fishing, hiking, canoeing, and skiing. In Sun Valley, Ernest taught Martha and his sons to hunt birds and antelope. Adventurous Martha was an ideal companion for this group of males, and Bumby remarked that his new stepmother was the first woman he had ever heard "use the 'f' word." The Heming-

For Whom the Bell Tolls became a feature film in 1943, starring Ingrid Bergman (left center) and Gary Cooper (right center).

ways stayed in Sun Valley as guests of Averell Harriman, a businessman and future governor of New York who owned property there. To gain publicity, Harriman offered movie stars and other well-known people rooms in his lodge at no charge.

The boys enjoyed unusual freedom when in their father's care. Ernest let them drink beer and hard liquor and sign for food and services at Harriman's lodge. Gregory, who turned nine in 1940, especially enjoyed getting massages, private skeet-shooting lessons, and gourmet meals merely by signing his name. He started drinking alcohol when he was eleven.

On January 31, 1941, Ernest and Martha voyaged to China. Eager to pursue her career as a war correspondent, Martha had signed on to cover the ongoing hostilities between China and Japan for *Collier's Magazine.* Ernest covered the war for *PM,* a liberal newspaper. The Chinese-Japanese War had begun in 1931, when the Japanese invaded Manchuria, in northeast China, securing railroads and other economic interests. Throughout the 1930s, the Japanese increased their fighting force in

China and seized more and more territory. By 1941, Japan controlled one-fourth of China, including most of the cities, factories, and transportation lines. A third of the Chinese people lived under Japanese control.

The Chinese were divided politically and militarily, with Communist forces under Mao Tse-tung opposing the Nationalist government of Chiang Kai-shek. Yet both sides fought to repel the invaders. Fierce, bloody battles took place between small bands of Chinese using old, rusted weapons and the well-organized Japanese soldiers, who were equipped with modern machine guns and artillery.

Martha and Ernest spent the first month of their trip in the British colony of Hong Kong, where they saw few signs of war and enjoyed good food and a comfortable hotel. They said good-bye to paved roads and cleanliness when they traveled north to the Seventh War Zone Head-quarters in Shaoguan. Tidy Martha developed an oozing fungal infection on her hands from the brackish water their hotel provided for washing. Ernest, who was used to rugged living, stayed dirty and disease free.

Clean, hot water flowed in Chongqing, the wartime capital, a city Ernest described as a "terraced, gray, bomb-spattered, fire-gutted, grim stone island." There, the Hemingways had lunch with Chiang Kai-shek and his wife, Soong Mei-ling, a woman who had been educated in the United States and who played a key role in Chinese politics.

Ernest saw many amazing sights in China, but nothing impressed him more than the spectacle of one hundred thousand workers building a military airfield by hand. In Sichuan Province, this "ragged, torn-clothed" army of laborers hauled away more than a million cubic meters of earth to level a thousand acres. They paved the runway with stone, mortar, and sand, and pulled ten-ton concrete rollers over the surface to flatten it. They sang a song with lyrics that meant "they work all day and all night to do this. They work all day and all night," Hemingway reported.

He and Martha were safely back in Cuba in July 1941, when Japan moved soldiers into French Indochina (present-day Vietnam). The Japanese were following the example of Nazi Germany, which had ruthlessly invaded Austria, Poland, Norway, Denmark, France, and other nations between 1938 and 1940. Great Britain alone fought to end Fascist dom-

Ernest and Martha chat with Soong Mei-ling, who was known to the world as Madame Chiang Kai-shek. The wife of the Nationalist Chinese leader had been educated in the United States and spoke fluent English.

ination of Europe. In an effort to halt Japan's aggression, President Franklin D. Roosevelt froze Japanese assets in the United States and halted the sale to Japan of oil and other materials needed for war. The Japanese retaliated on December 7, 1941, by launching a surprise attack on the U.S. naval base at Pearl Harbor, Hawaii, and drawing the United States into World War II. Americans entered the fight against Japan in the Pacific and against Germany and Italy in Europe and north Africa.

The fact that he had predicted this war brought Hemingway no satisfaction. "I have seen much war in my lifetime and I hate it profoundly," he said. "But there are worse things than war, and all of them come with defeat. The more you hate war, the more you know that once you are forced into it, for whatever reason it may be, you have to win it." Determined to do his small part for victory, Hemingway formed the "Crook Factory," a band of amateur spies, to track down Fascists working undercover in Havana, Cuba. This motley crew included fishermen, waiters, jai alai players, beach bums, Spanish expatriates, and a Catholic priest who had fought for the Loyalists in the Spanish Civil War. Ernest filed reports of his group's activities with the U.S. embassy in Havana, but the Crook Factory uncovered no real evidence of spies. Even so, their concern was not farfetched: Agents of Franco's government might well have been operating in Cuba, which had sided with the Allies in the war.

Hemingway next equipped the *Pilar* to search the Caribbean for German submarines. Again, the threat was real. The Germans, determined to stop shipments of oil and bauxite (aluminum ore) from leaving the Caribbean and the Gulf of Mexico, had sunk 263 ships in the region by November 1942. Ernest and his accomplices planned to disguise themselves as scientists studying the region's biology. If an enemy U-boat stopped them, then they would sink it in a surprise attack. Dazzled by Hemingway's fame, officers of the U.S. Navy supplied machine guns, hand grenades, and other weapons for this project without stopping to think if it could possibly work. Ernest grew a bushy sea captain's beard and spent many days patrolling the warm waters of the Gulf Stream. Patrick and Gregory joined the expedition during a summer visit in 1942. The Nazi hunters claimed to have spotted several German subs, but none ever came into firing range.

Ernest continued to drink heavily, both at sea and on land. From the *Pilar,* he practiced throwing grenades into the water. At home, his insults and sudden explosions of rage frightened away friends who had once found him charming. He cared for many cats that roamed freely through the rooms at Finca Vigía, whether or not they were house trained.

Martha flew to London in November 1943 to report on conditions in wartime Britain for *Collier's Magazine.* Lonely in her absence, Ernest demanded to know if she was a reporter or the wife who slept in his bed. When Martha came home for a visit in March 1944, she pressured Ernest to get an overseas writing assignment, too. She thought that by covering the war together, they could recapture the excitement they had felt in Spain. Also, she was convinced a change of scenery and a new purpose would do her husband good. Ernest at last agreed. One morning, he announced to Martha that he would be covering the war in Europe for *Collier's.* He had offered the editors his services, and they had hired him on the spot. Because the U.S. War Department allowed only one reporter from each magazine or newspaper at the front, he had stolen her job.

Shocked, angry, and deeply hurt, Martha Gellhorn decided then and there to end her marriage to Ernest Hemingway. She went to Europe and reported on World War II, although she lacked official press credentials, and became one of the leading war correspondents of the twentieth century.

The months Hemingway spent in Europe, from May 1944 through January 1945, were a time of emotional highs, recklessness, and adventure. He did his best to live in the "now." The excitement began right away, when he reached war-torn London. In a crowded restaurant, he met Mary Welsh, the London correspondent for *Time* magazine. This small, spirited Minnesota native was dining with another writer, Irwin Shaw, but this did not stop Ernest from asking her to have lunch with him soon. Mary saw that "Above the great, bushy, brindled beard, his eyes were beautiful," and she accepted his invitation. Days later, Ernest surprised

Hemingway was photographed in a full beard for the identity card he carried while reporting on World War II in Europe.

her by saying, "I don't know you, Mary. But I want to marry you." He had to be kidding—or so Mary thought until his frequent letters and efforts to see her proved he was sincere.

A week after meeting Mary, Ernest saw his brother at a party hosted by Robert Capa, whose photographs of the Spanish Civil War had made him world famous. Leicester was serving in Europe with a documentary film unit. Later that night, some English friends drove Ernest back to his hotel. Maneuvering through streets darkened by the wartime blackout proved treacherous, and the driver smashed into a steel water tank. The collision sent Ernest headfirst through the windshield; he suffered a concussion and needed fifty-seven stitches in his scalp.

Hemingway writes in a London hotel room in 1944, while covering World War II for *Collier's Magazine.*

Despite bandages and lingering headaches, on the night of June 5, Hemingway boarded the *Dorothea L. Dix,* the transport ship that carried journalists across the English Channel to witness the historic landing of Allied troops at Normandy. As the beach came into view, he climbed into an LCV(P) landing craft, a "floating cigar box" just big enough to hold a platoon of thirty-six men. Hemingway described for *Collier's* the roar of the 225-horsepower diesel engines, the flash "like a blast furnace" that issued from the fourteen-inch guns of the nearby battleship *Texas,* and the unsmiling faces of GIs about to be put ashore. He also gave his readers the false impression that the landing craft's crew depended on his help to stay on course.

Mary Welsh covered World War II in London for *Time* magazine.

By mid-July, Hemingway was well enough to follow the American forces that were pushing deeper into France, freeing towns and villages from Nazi occupation. He briefly attached himself to the 22nd Infantry Regiment, which was commanded by Colonel Charles T. Lanham, a career army officer.

Hemingway called Buck Lanham "the finest and bravest and most intelligent military commander I have known." Lanham wrote poems and short stories and hoped to learn something about writing from this famous author. Hemingway had no patience for discussing his craft, though, and kept asking about courage. "That is all he wanted to talk about," Lanham said. "Courage for me was something I happened to be born with. Luck and courage. . . . I told him courage is not what a sober person discusses in public."

"We have had a tough, fine time. This is the 8th day we have been attacking all the time," Hemingway wrote to Mary, his "Small Friend," on August 1. Three days later, he sustained another concussion when he was riding in the sidecar of a motorcycle that was speeding along on a curving road. As they came around a bend, the driver had to brake hard to avoid hitting a German antitank gun. Hemingway struck his head when he was thrown into a ditch. This head injury gave him double vision, slowed speech, and ringing in the ears that lasted for months.

As the Allies moved toward Paris, Hemingway made the village of Rambouillet his base of operations. He secured weapons for a band of French partisans who were fighting to free their country from Nazi occupation, and he grilled local citizens about German troop activity in the region. The Geneva Convention, the international set of rules for the conduct of war, prohibits journalists from bearing arms, so Colonel David Bruce issued handwritten orders giving Hemingway command of the partisans. Bruce commented that in military affairs, Hemingway "was a real expert, especially in regard to guerilla activities and to intelligence collection." Nevertheless, Hemingway had to explain his actions to the Third Army Court of Inquiry in October 1944.

From Rambouillet, he and his band followed the American armored column into Paris. At a turn in the road, Hemingway's throat choked up with emotion, and he paused to clean his glasses, "because there now,

Parisians celebrate their liberation from Nazi control.

below us, gray and always beautiful, was the city I love best in all the world," he wrote. The liberation of Paris was a joyous event, a time for waving flags and uncorking bottles of champagne. Parisians welcomed the Americans with flowers and kisses, and everywhere people shouted, *"Vive la France!"*—"Long live France!" Hemingway liked to boast that he liberated the bar at the Ritz Hotel by being the first American to order drinks there since Nazi tanks had rolled into the city in 1940.

That fall Hemingway left the safety of Paris to come under fire alongside Colonel Buck Lanham, who was leading his forces into Belgium. Hemingway was with Lanham and the 22nd Infantry for the Hürtgen Forest campaign, the longest series of battles ever fought by the U.S. Army. The campaign began on September 19, 1944, and continued through February 10, 1945. Progress was slow in this thickly wooded region, the fighting was fierce, and losses were high. Rifles were useless against heavy bombardment from German artillery; soldiers hugged tree trunks as shells exploded overhead. "It was brutal," said a veteran of the campaign. "You'd look around, you couldn't see far because the forest was so dark. But you could make out medics scurrying around." The 22nd lost 85 percent of its men while taking just one village and six thousand yards of forest.

The shells missed Hemingway, but constant exposure to snow, mud, and fog gave him pneumonia. While recovering in Paris, he learned that Bumby had been captured behind enemy lines. At age twenty-one, Ernest's oldest son had been serving in Europe with the Office of Strategic Services, the government's wartime intelligence agency. He would spend six months in a German prison camp but would come through the war unharmed.

Ernest waited out the closing months of World War II in Cuba. He divorced Martha, and on March 14, 1946, he married Mary. On June 16, 1947, at the American embassy in Havana, the U.S. government awarded him the Bronze Star for heroism in Europe. The honor was a bright moment in a dark period of drinking, ill health, and frustration. He started to write a novel called *The Garden of Eden,* which dealt with a bisexual love triangle, a daring and different theme for Ernest Hemingway. As he typed page after page, the manuscript swelled into a bulging, unmanageable mass of words. It grew to thirty, forty, and finally forty-eight chapters, but he could not figure out how to finish it. He never would. In 1947, Max Perkins died of pneumonia, believing that "Hemingway is through."

Hemingway had lost one of his "best and most loyal friends and wisest counselors." He felt renewed inspiration, though, in 1948, when he and Mary traveled to Italy. There, they met nineteen-year-old Adriana Ivancich, who belonged to an aristocratic family in Venice. At forty-nine, Ernest fell in love with Adriana's youth and beauty, although to her he was never more than a dear, older friend. He told her, "You have given me back the possibility of writing again, and I shall be grateful to you for it always." He gave Adriana's face to Renata, a character in his next novel, *Across the River and Into the Trees*.

Hemingway chats with Adriana Ivancich during her visit to Finca Vigía in late 1950 and early 1951.

Much of the action in Hemingway's sixth published novel takes place in the mind of Colonel Richard Cantwell, a fifty-one-year-old American army officer stationed in Italy. Cantwell is dying very gradually of a heart ailment; during a day of duck hunting, he recalls the most memorable events of his life, including scenes of war and a weekend spent in Venice with Renata, the young woman he loves and who loves him.

Across the River and Into the Trees contains sections of beautiful writing, but the literary world dismissed it as Hemingway's worst novel. Reviewers described it with words like embarrassing, artificial, and boring. E. B. White, a well-known essayist and the future author of *Charlotte's Web,* wrote a stinging parody titled "Across the Street and Into the Grill."

Hemingway threw temper tantrums and once again ranted about the critics who were out to destroy him. As it turned out, he was not quite through, washed up, or even down for the count. He still had one great book to write.

ELEVEN

Out Where No One Can Help

In 1948, Hemingway began three related stories inspired by the land, air, and sea. They all featured a character named Thomas Hudson, an artist with a house on Bimini, and together they were to make up a novel. The work progressed slowly and painfully until January 1951, when he sat down to write another story. This one told of an old Cuban fisherman who ventures far from land and hooks an enormous fish. Suddenly, Hemingway wrote easily and joyfully, as he had when he was young. He finished the story and gave it a simple title, *The Old Man and the Sea,* to match the plain, straightforward language he had used to write it. He thought about adding it to the book about Thomas Hudson, perhaps placing it at the end.

Mary typed the new story from Ernest's handwritten pages, just as Sunny and Pauline had typed *A Farewell to Arms.* As she read about the old man battling alone against nature, she felt the tiny hairs on her forearms rise. The fisherman's story was good—much too good to be tacked onto something else, she said. It needed to be published on its own. The editors at Scribner's agreed. And not only would they bring out the story in book form, but also *Life* magazine planned to print it in a single issue, on September 1, 1952.

More than five million people read the story in *Life,* and hundreds of thousands bought the book, keeping it on bestseller lists for more than six months. Praise poured in from around the world. "His best. Time may show it to be the best single piece of any of us, I mean his and my contemporaries," declared the American novelist William Faulkner. A critic for the *Times* of London also pronounced it "the best story Hemingway has ever written."

The Old Man and the Sea touched readers' hearts as no other book by Hemingway had ever done. In the story of Santiago the fisherman, the most ordinary of Hemingway's heroes, people sensed something mythical. They discovered life's basic struggle in this tale of a human being who reaches for something great.

Santiago lives alone in a shack on the Cuban coast. His only friend is a boy named Manolin, and he has gone many days without catching a fish. Hoping to change his luck, he ventures "too far out," in search of something big. Leaving his fellow fishermen in safer waters, he hooks a marlin that is longer and heavier than any ever caught. The powerful fish puts up a fight and pulls the boat and the fisherman beyond the sight of land. Santiago needs all his strength and stamina to hold on to the marlin, but at last he kills it and lashes it to his boat.

Then the sharks come. Lured by the scent of blood, they circle the small boat and dart forward to tear great bites from the marlin's flesh. Santiago fights back, but he cannot win. He is exhausted by the time he reaches shore, when only the bones of the immense fish are left. "But man is not made for defeat," the old man knows. "A man can be destroyed but not defeated." Santiago has failed, but he will go on living. He will rest and fish again, with Manolin beside him.

Ernest and Mary were themselves fishing in early May 1953 when they heard on the *Pilar*'s radio that Ernest Hemingway had won the Pulitzer Prize in fiction for *The Old Man and the Sea*. This was his first important award in his many years of writing. In 1941, the selection committee had voted to give him the prize for *For Whom the Bell Tolls,* but the president of Columbia University, the institution that awards the Pulitzer Prizes, vetoed the choice. He refused to honor "a work of this nature,"

Ernest communes with a favorite cat, Cristobal Colón, at Finca Vigía.

he said, one featuring obscene language and sexual content. Columbia awarded no prize for fiction that year.

The early 1950s were a time of professional success and personal loss. In June 1951, Grace Hemingway died in Memphis, Tennessee, where she had gone to live with Sunny and her family. Ernest stayed away from the funeral, just as he had stayed away from Grace throughout his adult life. But leafing through the scrapbooks she had filled with mementoes of his childhood, he remembered fondly the mother he had known before wounded feelings and anger drove him away from her. Then, less than four months later, Pauline died suddenly from a rare tumor of the adrenal gland. "I loved her very much for many years and the hell with her faults," Ernest said bigheartedly, but he blamed the death on their son Gregory, whose recent arrest for drug possession had upset Pauline.

In 1953, Ernest returned with Mary to a place he had loved with Pauline: east Africa. Upon reaching Kenya in late August, he had a happy reunion with Philip Percival, his guide so many years earlier. He managed to kill a rhinoceros, a lion, a leopard, and other animals, but his heavy drinking and sloppy shooting marred the hunting. Percival spoke honestly, telling his old friend, "The whole thing has been a disgrace!"

Ernest gave up the hunt and found contentment in sightseeing and reading the many books and magazines he had brought from home. He also wrote about his experiences for *Look* magazine. On January 21, 1954, he and Mary hired a pilot named Roy Marsh to take them up in a small plane, so they could admire the magnificent landscape from above. They flew over the Ngorongoro Crater, a huge depression in the earth that was formed when a colossal volcano exploded millions of years ago, and over the breathtaking Ruwenzori Mountains, along the western border of Uganda. They were circling Murchison Falls, where the Nile River plunges more than one hundred forty feet, when Marsh dipped low to avoid a flock of ibis. The plane struck a telegraph wire and crash-landed in thick vegetation.

Ernest escaped with a sprained shoulder and Mary broke two ribs, but their pilot was uninjured. They spent a night together in the bush

Ernest and Mary visit
a Masai village. The
Masai people of east
Africa are renowned
for raising cattle.

before flagging down a passing riverboat that was headed for the Ugandan city of Butiaba. There, they learned that a British pilot had spotted the wreckage of their plane but reported seeing no survivors. Word had gone out to the world that Ernest Hemingway was dead. That very day, Americans were reading his obituary in their newspapers.

A man named Reginald Cartwright, who had been searching for their bodies in his own small plane, volunteered to fly the Hemingways and Marsh to the larger city of Entebbe. The four climbed into Cartwright's aged aircraft and proceeded down the dusty, bumpy airstrip "in the manner of a wild goat," Ernest observed. The plane lurched into the air and flew briefly before falling to the ground and bursting into flames. Roy Marsh kicked out a window, and he and Mary escaped easily, although

Mary had hurt her knee in the crash. Cartwright also kicked out a window and freed himself. Ernest, however, panicked when he tried the plane's door and found it stuck. He butted the windshield with his head until he broke it, and emerged from the crash with internal injuries and a head wound severe enough to leak cranial fluid. The resulting concussion caused double vision and vomiting.

He was still recovering when he and Mary visited Patrick and his wife, Henrietta (Henny), who were living on a farm in Tanganyika. Despite pain and unsteadiness, Ernest felt compelled to show his courage when a brush fire broke out nearby. While aiding the firefighters, he fell onto the flames, subjecting his battered body to second- and third-degree burns.

Ernest rested in Italy before showing Mary the Spanish countryside that had served as the setting of *For Whom the Bell Tolls*. He went home

As an African guide looks on, Hemingway inspects a cape buffalo he has killed.

A Cuban official pins the Order of Carlos Manuel de Céspedes, his government's highest honor, to Hemingway's lapel on the writer's fifty-fifth birthday, July 21, 1954. The medal was named for a hero of the nineteenth-century struggle for Cuban independence from Spain.

with her to Cuba and learned, on October 28, 1954, that he had won the Nobel Prize for literature. The Nobel Prizes are the most prestigious awards in the world. The Swedish Academy, the organization that selects the winners in literature, had recognized Hemingway "For his mastery of the art of narrative, most recently demonstrated in *The Old Man and the Sea,* and for the influence that he has exerted on contemporary style."

Too ill to travel to Stockholm to accept the prize, Hemingway wrote a speech that was read aloud at the award banquet by the U.S. ambassador to Sweden, John M. Cabot. In his brief statement, Hemingway returned to the theme of *The Old Man and the Sea:* "How simple the writing of literature would be if it were only necessary to write in another way what has been well written. It is because we have had such great writers in the past that a writer is driven far out past where he can go, out to where no one can help him." The Swedish ambassador to Cuba presented the prize to Hemingway at Finca Vigía.

To have the world acknowledge the value of his work pleased Hemingway, but to think that he had lost his creative power frightened him.

He tried to write a book about his second African safari, but he put words on paper endlessly, not knowing when to stop. He gratefully wrapped the monstrous manuscript in plastic when the time came to advise the crew that was making a movie of *The Old Man and the Sea* or to travel in Europe with Mary.

In Paris, Ernest received a Christmas surprise in 1956, when the staff of the Ritz Hotel presented him with two trunks he had left there in 1928. Opening this forgotten luggage was like peering into a time capsule. Ernest took out clothes he had last worn twenty-eight years before, yellowed newspaper clippings, notebooks filled with his early efforts at writing, and a stash of typed fiction. The stories Hadley had lost remained missing, but Ernest was reminded of his happy life with her and Bumby. He brought these treasures home to Cuba and again started a rambling writing project, a memoir of his life in Paris.

In 1959, Hemingway prepared to leave Cuba, another place he loved. In that year, revolutionaries led by Fidel Castro overthrew the nation's leader, Fulgencio Batista. They executed their enemies, seized property, and robbed Cubans of their civil liberties. Ernest and Mary bought a house in Ketchum, Idaho, near Sun Valley and far from the Cuban revolution. It was a concrete block a mile out of town that Gregory Hemingway called "an ideal buttress against the world, and as safe a refuge as could be found for a paranoid."

Paranoid. In Cuba, Ernest hid childhood photographs of himself, fearing Mary would secretly sell them. In Idaho restaurants, he suspected that customers at other tables were FBI agents who had come to spy on him. He was sure the Internal Revenue Service was after him, too, and riding in a car, he worried that the driver might be planning to kill him. Watching a television production of *Macbeth,* a drama filled with plotting and murder, became too much to bear.

Despite both mental and physical decline, Ernest went to Spain with Mary in 1959, to report on the summer's bullfighting for *Life* magazine. The season promised to be exciting, with two up-and-coming bullfighters dueling *mano a mano* (hand to hand). In each of several matches, the men would fight six bulls to decide who was the better matador. Wherever the

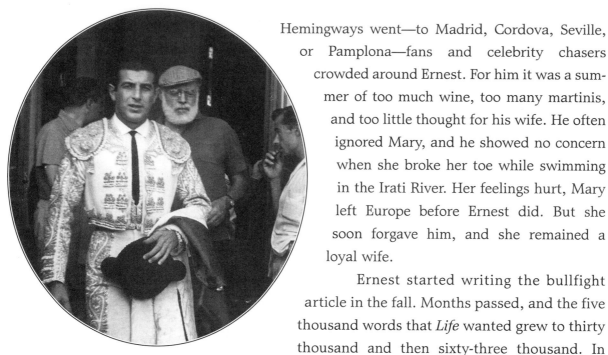

Hemingway walks behind Antonio Ordóñez, one of two matadors who dueled *mano a mano* in 1959. His father, Cayetano Ordóñez, had dedicated a bull to Hadley in 1925.

Hemingways went—to Madrid, Cordova, Seville, or Pamplona—fans and celebrity chasers crowded around Ernest. For him it was a summer of too much wine, too many martinis, and too little thought for his wife. He often ignored Mary, and he showed no concern when she broke her toe while swimming in the Irati River. Her feelings hurt, Mary left Europe before Ernest did. But she soon forgave him, and she remained a loyal wife.

Ernest started writing the bullfight article in the fall. Months passed, and the five thousand words that *Life* wanted grew to thirty thousand and then sixty-three thousand. In late May 1960, when Hemingway announced that he had written more than a hundred thousand words, the editors at *Life* demanded that he cut seventy thousand of them. Hemingway pored over the pages but found only about five hundred words he could do without. A younger writer named A. E. Hotchner helped him trim away more than half the manuscript, and *Life* published the piece, called "The Dangerous Summer," the following September. For Hemingway, the process had been a nightmare. "I act cheerful like always but am not," he told Hotchner. "I'm bone tired and very beat up emotionally."

Stories mirror lives. In *Death in the Afternoon,* Hemingway wrote that "all stories, if continued far enough, end in death, and he is no true-story teller who would keep that from you." His own decline toward death hastened in late 1960. Suffering greatly from skyrocketing blood pressure, kidney and liver ailments, and mental illness, he entered the Mayo Clinic, a world-famous hospital complex in Rochester, Minnesota, under a false name in order to protect his privacy. The physicians in Rochester subjected him to a course of shock therapy, using an electric current to bring on seizures in a process that had been shown to relieve depression and delusional thinking.

The treatments allowed Hemingway to leave the hospital, but they wiped away memories and left him unable to write. When he was invited to prepare a very brief tribute to the newly elected president, John F. Kennedy, the task took a week and brought him to tears. His trademark, the simple declarative sentence, had become too hard for him to compose.

Hemingway hardly ever saw visitors in Ketchum; Dr. George Saviers, who stopped in each day to check his blood pressure, was an exception. Saviers arrived on Friday, April 21, to find Ernest in the sitting room,

Hemingway, looking old and ill, stands outside Finca Vigía, his Cuban home.

Friends and family called Hemingway's house in Ketchum, Idaho, bleak, but its mountain view inspired awe.

wearing a bathrobe and holding a shotgun and two shells. Mary was speaking softly to him, trying to keep him from doing something desperate. Saviers and Mary got the gun away from him and took him to a hospital, where he was sedated, but as soon as he was home, he tried to shoot himself.

Saviers arranged to have his famous patient readmitted to the Mayo Clinic and transported there by plane. When the small aircraft stopped to refuel in Rapid City, South Dakota, Hemingway climbed out to stretch. But he soon started walking toward another plane that was taxiing down the runway, and some witnesses thought he planned to walk straight into a spinning propeller. The pilot turned off the engine, so whether Hemingway intended to end his life in this way will never be known.

Dr. Howard P. Rome, Ernest's psychiatrist at the Mayo Clinic, prescribed another round of shock treatment. Ernest's outlook improved, and he spoke frankly with Dr. Rome about his fears, his need to feel free, and his desire to be trusted. On June 26, Rome trusted Hemingway enough to let him go home. "My hope and intention was to do something for him," Rome stated. "I truly felt that the risks were negligible and that he and his future [were] worth all of them and more besides."

Mary doubted that Ernest was ready to leave the hospital, but she brought him home to Ketchum. On Sunday, July 2, he woke early. While Mary slept, he found her keys and unlocked the basement cabinet that held his guns. He carried one to the foyer, loaded it, and shot himself in the head.

Ernest Hemingway spent his final months in isolation, both physically and emotionally.

Months passed before Mary could face the truth about what had happened. "Not consciously lying, I told the press that the shooting had been accidental," she said.

Archibald MacLeish saw nothing accidental in the suicide and was moved to write a poem. "Death explains, / That kind of death," he wrote. He imagined looking backward in time through Hemingway's life, at scenes of Idaho, Africa, Spain, and Paris, as if watching a film that was being rewound. He revealed that through this violent death, he better understood the old friend he had lost:

> The gun between the teeth explains.
> The shattered mouth foretells the singing boy.

EPILOGUE

Remembering

Hemingway enjoys a day of fishing in Key West.

One of the greatest writers of the twentieth century had died in a terrible, violent way. Many people needed to say something, to comment on the life Hemingway had lived. "Few Americans had a greater impact on the emotions and attitudes of the American people than Ernest Hemingway," said President John F. Kennedy. "Although his journeys throughout the world—to France, to Spain, and even Africa—made him one of the great citizens of the world, he ended life as he began it, in the heartland of America."

Lowell Thomas, a journalist and adventurer who had met Hemingway, relived happy memories: "Who will ever forget 'Papa,' with his grizzled beard, reminiscing about his roistering days as a Bohemian in the Paris Latin Quarter? Who will forget the way he used to talk about the bullfighters he knew?"

Homer Croy, a writer, was not alone in voicing a harsher view. "Put me down as no admirer of Hemingway," he said. "He killed his first wild animals when he was twelve and he kept consistently at it until he killed himself. . . . That was Hemingway—kill, kill, kill!" Hemingway remained controversial, even in death.

The family held a small, private funeral in Ketchum, to which they invited a few friends. Mary was there, and so were Ernest's three sons. His siblings were present, all but Carol, who could not attend. At the graveside, a Catholic priest read lines from the section of Ecclesiastes that had inspired the title *The Sun Also Rises*. Then Ernest Miller Hemingway was buried between two evergreens, facing the Sawtooth Mountains. It comforted the people who loved him to imagine him looking always at this breathtaking landscape.

Hemingway had left behind several unfinished and unpublished works, and these began to appear as books. The first of his posthumous novels, *Islands in the Stream,* was issued in 1970. Mary Hemingway and publisher Charles Scribner assembled this book from the "sea" section of Hemingway's projected three-part novel about the artist Thomas Hudson. Hemingway never did write the "land" and "air" sections that he had planned.

The Dangerous Summer, Hemingway's account of the 1959 bullfighting season, was published as a book in 1985, and *The Garden of Eden,* his bisexual love story, was released a year later. To produce the latter book, an editor at Scribner's chopped away most of Hemingway's 200,000 words and was left with a slim volume.

Two versions of Hemingway's novel based on his second African safari have been published. The first was *True at First Light,* edited by Patrick Hemingway, in 1999. The second version, *Under Kilimanjaro,* contains the author's complete text and became available in 2005.

As a fiction writer, Hemingway often could not resist changing details or even inventing whole scenes to make a nonfiction account more compelling than it would have been had he left the truth alone. For this reason, his memoir of Paris, *A Moveable Feast,* which was published in 1964, contains passages that may well have been born in his imagination. The writer Nancy Milford has reminded readers that the accuracy of Hemingway's account is unimportant, because the book has much to teach about his character. She explained, "Hemingway's memoir was the way he *wanted* to remember his past."

NOTES

Young Ernest Hemingway writes during a fishing trip on Walloon Lake, 1916.

All books and articles cited in the notes are listed in the bibliography. In addition, the following abbreviations have been used:

JFK Ernest Hemingway Collection, John F. Kennedy Presidential Library

LILLY Hemingway Collection, Lilly Library, Indiana University

Chapter 1. The Whole World, Boiled Down

p. 1 Hemingway, "I was trying to learn . . ." is from E. Hemingway, *Death in the Afternoon,* p. 2.

p. 3 Hemingway, "The bullfight was so far . . ." is from E. Hemingway, *Death,* p. 3.

p. 5 Hemingway, "If a man is making . . ." is from E. Hemingway, "Monologue to the Maestro," p. 21.

p. 5 Hemingway, "It is a perpetual challenge . . ." is from Baker 1981, p. 419.

p. 5 Hemingway, "If I started to write . . ." is from E. Hemingway, *A Moveable Feast,* p. 12.

p. 6   Butcher, "There is no flesh . . ." is from Butcher, p. 11.

p. 6   Beach, "You can't open a novel . . ." is from Beach, p. 81.

p. 6   Hemingway, "I am trying to make . . ." is from Baker 1981, p. 397.

Chapter 2. "A Fine Big Manly Fellow"

p. 7   Hall, "Mark my words . . ." is quoted in Baker 1969, p. 7.

p. 7   Bagley, "The Hemingways have a boy!" is quoted in Guarino, p. 86.

p. 8   Grace Hemingway, "two summer girls," is from Grace Hemingway's
         scrapbooks, vol. 1. JFK.

p. 9   Clarence E. Hemingway, "Mr. Tom Cat turned . . ." is quoted in Baker
         1969, p. 10.

p. 10   Marcelline Hemingway, "Daddy could make any walk . . ." is quoted in
         Guarino, p. 86.

p. 10   Grace Hemingway, "When asked what he is afraid of . . ." is quoted in
         Tessitore, p. 25.

p. 12   Grace Hemingway, "It's not the kind of book . . ." is quoted in Guarino,
         p. 86.

p. 12   Sampson, "We cooked the haunches . . ." is quoted in Sanford, p. 81.

p. 12   Adams [Hemingway], "I can blow him to hell. . . ." is from
         E. Hemingway, *The Complete Short Stories of Ernest Hemingway,*
         p. 375.

p. 13   Hemingway, "I desire to do pioneering . . ." is from E. Hemingway, high
         school notebook, JFK.

p. 13   Clarence E. Hemingway, "You have grown to be . . ." is quoted in Baker
         1969, p. 20.

p. 13   Marcelline Hemingway, "We girls watched . . ." is from Sanford, p. 137.

p. 14   "Ernie was a handsome boy . . ." is quoted in Nagel, p. 23.

p. 15   Hemingway, "I thought he was the best . . ." is from E. Hemingway,
         "Letter to a Young Writer," p. 10.

p. 15   Walpole, "'Tisn't life that matters! . . ." is from Walpole, p. 11.

p. 16   Walpole, "Make of me a man . . ." is from Walpole, p. 484.

p. 16   Hemingway, "save My-in-gau, the wolf . . ." is from Maziarka and
         Vogel, p. 94.

p. 16   Hemingway, "like a shaggy thunderbolt" and "wolf jaws," are from
         Maziarka and Vogel, p. 100.

p. 16   Lardner, "I promised the Wife . . ." is from Lardner, p. 159.

p. 16   Hemingway, "Evanston wasn't no meat . . ." is from Bruccoli 1971,
         p. 49.

p. 19   Hemingway, "noted lady veterinarian," is from Maziarka and Vogel,
         p. 111.

p. 20   Jordan [Hemingway], "His father had been . . ." is from E. Hemingway,
         For Whom the Bell Tolls, pp. 405–6.

Chapter 3. Into the Furnace of Suffering

p. 22   Crouse, "He had the wonderful habit . . ." is quoted in Fenton, p. 33.

p. 22   Wellington, "Use short sentences. . . ." is quoted in Fenton, p. 31.

p. 22   Hemingway, "Those were the best rules . . ." is quoted in Fenton,
         pp. 35–36.

p. 22   Hemingway, "shady characters," is quoted in Fenton, p. 35.

p. 23   Wellington, "He always wanted to be . . ." is quoted in Fenton, p. 34.

p. 23   Hemingway, "something alive about each one," is from an unpublished,
         undated sketch of Lionel Moise, p. 1. JFK.

p. 23   Moise, "The only way to improve . . ." is quoted in Fenton, p. 40.

p. 23   Edgar, "the romance of newspaper work," is quoted in Baker 1969,
         p. 33.

p. 24   Hemingway, "Now mother I got awfully angry . . ." is from Baker 1981,
         p. 4.

p. 26   Hemingway, "think of what the rottenest . . ." and "heaved but four
         times" are from Baker 1981, p. 9.

p. 26   Brumback, "as if he'd been sent . . ." is from Brumback, p. 2C.

p. 26   Hemingway, "I must admit, frankly . . ." is from E. Hemingway, *Death,*
         p. 136.

p. 28   Hemingway, "There's nothing here but scenery . . ." is quoted in
         Brumback, p. 2C.

p. 28   Italian Supreme Command, "furnace of suffering," is from Supreme
         Command of the Royal Italian Army, p. 81.

p. 29   Brumback, "The Italians in the trenches . . ." is in a letter from
         Theodore Brumback to Clarence Edmonds Hemingway, July 14,
         1918. LILLY.

p. 30   Hemingway, *"chuh—chuh—chuh—chuh,"* "I tried to breathe . . . ," and
         "The ground was torn up . . ." are from E. Hemingway, *A Farewell
         to Arms,* p. 54.

p. 30   Hemingway, "like a sharp smack . . ." and "coat and pants looked
         like . . ." are from Baker 1981, p. 14.

p. 30   Hemingway, "How much better to die . . ." is from Baker 1981, p. 19.

p. 31   Hemingway, "hurting like 227 little devils . . ." and "The Italian surgeon did a peach . . ." are from Baker 1981, p. 15.

p. 31   Hemingway, "This is a peach of a hospital . . ." is from Baker 1981, p. 12.

p. 31   Hemingway, "Milan is a peach of a town," is in a letter from Ernest Hemingway to Grace Hall Hemingway, July 29, 1918. LILLY.

p. 31   Hemingway, "It's the next best thing . . ." is from Baker 1981, p. 13.

p. 32   Macdonald, *"like a good mother"* and "dear broken doll," are in a letter from Elsie Macdonald to Ernest Hemingway, December 14, 1926. JFK.

p. 33   American Medical Association, "the greatest enemy of all," is from "Editorial," p. 2154.

p. 33   von Kurowsky, "The Light of My Existence . . ." is quoted in Baker 1969, p. 52.

p. 34   Hemingway, "I've only got about 50 . . ." is from Baker 1981, p. 20.

Chapter 4. A Stranger at Home

p. 35   "any other man, in or out . . ." is quoted in Lynn, p. 96.

p. 35   von Kurowsky, "How I wish I knew . . ." is quoted in Baker 1969, p. 57.

p. 37   "punctured trousers," is quoted in Bruccoli 1986, p. 4.

p. 38   Harold Krebs and his mother [Hemingway], "But the world they were in . . . ," "God has some work . . . ," "I'm not in His Kingdom," "Don't you love your mother . . . ," and "No," are from E. Hemingway, *In Our Time,* pp. 94–99.

p. 38   Hemingway, "That's all shut behind me," is from Baker 1981, p. 25.

p. 38   "There's a cripple . . ." is quoted in Baker 1969, p. 63.

p. 40   Hemingway, "Circulating Pictures," is from White, p. 3.

p. 40   Clarence E. Hemingway, "vitriolistic words," is quoted in Baker 1969, p. 71.

p. 40   Leicester Hemingway, "Downy snipe feathers . . ." is from L. Hemingway, p. 70.

p. 41   Grace Hemingway, "Ernest called me every name . . ." is quoted in Reynolds, p. 136.

p. 41   Grace Hemingway, "Unless you, my son . . ." is quoted in Lynn, p. 118.

p. 42   Clarence E. Hemingway, "get busy and make his own way . . ." is quoted in Baker 1969, p. 73.

p. 43   Anderson, "The writer, an old man . . ." is from Anderson 1995, p. 1.

p. 43   Anderson, "a young fellow of extraordinary talent," is from Anderson

1953, p. 82.

p. 43   Anderson, "an American writer instinctively . . ." is from Anderson
1953, p. 85.

p. 43   Richardson, "a pair of very red cheeks . . ." is quoted in Baker 1969,
p. 76.

p. 43   Hemingway, "I knew she was the girl . . ." is quoted in L. Hemingway,
p. 71.

p. 45   Hemingway, "Merry Christmas to you . . ." is from Baker 1981, p. 43.

p. 45   Bradfield, "a beautiful youth," and "was immensely flattering . . ." are
quoted in Baker 1969, p. 78.

p. 45   Richardson, "The world's a jail . . ." is quoted in Baker 1969, p. 79.

p. 45   Hemingway, "for a little while at least," is quoted in Baker 1969, p. 77.

p. 45   Hemingway, "guy loves a couple or three streams . . ." is from Baker
1981, p. 48.

p. 46   Richardson, "I was dull in St. Louis . . ." is quoted in Kert, p. 94.

p. 46   Leicester Hemingway, "moving from side to side . . ." is from
L. Hemingway, p. 73.

p. 46   Anderson, "wholeheartedly and without reservation," is quoted in
Fanning, p. 7.

Chapter 5. True Sentences

p. 48   Hemingway, "cold and damp but crowded . . ." is from Baker 1981,
p. 60.

p. 48   Hemingway, "sad, evilly run café . . ." is from E. Hemingway,
Moveable, p. 3.

p. 48   Hemingway, "All you have to do . . ." and "It was easy then . . ." are
from E. Hemingway, *Moveable,* p. 12.

p. 49   [caption] "There are many black dresses . . ." is from "The Traveler's
Paris of To-Day," p. 625.

p. 49   Hemingway, "a small, steep country . . ." is from White, p. 18.

p. 50   Hemingway, "You are sitting absolutely . . ." is from E. Hemingway,
Dateline Toronto, p. 110.

p. 50   Hemingway, "She was kind, cheerful . . ." is from E. Hemingway,
Moveable, p. 35.

p. 52   Stein, "There is a great deal . . ." is from G. Stein, p. 213.

p. 52   Hemingway, "He habitually leads . . ." and "Pound sweats well . . ."
are from Baker 1981, p. 62.

p. 52   Hemingway, "developed a terrific wallop," is from Baker 1981, p. 65.

p. 53   Hemingway, "a big, jolly, middle-western . . ." is from White, p. 31.

p. 53   Eastman, "a modest and princely-mannered . . ." is from Eastman
            1959, p. 45.

p. 53   Hemingway, "like a tuba player . . ." is from E. Hemingway, *Dateline,*
            p. 145.

p. 53   Hemingway, "a country grocery storekeeper . . ." is from
            E. Hemingway, *Dateline,* p. 147.

p. 54   Hemingway, "far and away the best . . ." is from E. Hemingway,
            Dateline, p. 146.

p. 54   Hemingway, "a brood of dragons' teeth" and "no distinction between
            Socialists . . ." are from E. Hemingway, *Dateline,* p. 131.

p. 54   Hadley Hemingway, "a human blister," is from Kert, p. 120.

p. 55   Hemingway, "big, brown-faced man . . ." and Mussolini, "We have
            enough force . . ." are from E. Hemingway, *Dateline,* p. 172.

p. 56   Hemingway, "rain-furrowed and dull," is from E. Hemingway, *Dateline,*
            p. 177.

p. 56   Hemingway, "Chasing yesterdays . . ." is from E. Hemingway, *Dateline,*
            p. 180.

p. 56   Hemingway, "like going into the empty gloom . . ." is from
            E. Hemingway, *Dateline,* p. 176.

p. 57   Hemingway, "Constantinople is noisy . . ." is quoted in Baker 1969,
            p. 97.

p. 57   Hemingway, "dirty, tired, unshaven, wind-bitten," is from
            E. Hemingway, *Dateline,* p. 245.

p. 57   "It is better than sleeping . . ." is from E. Hemingway, *Dateline,*
            p. 250.

p. 58   Hemingway, "never-ending, staggering march," is from E. Hemingway,
            Dateline, p. 232.

p. 58   Hemingway, "It was true all right . . ." is from E. Hemingway,
            Moveable, p. 74.

p. 61   Hemingway, "There are never any suicides . . ." is from E. Hemingway,
            88 Poems, p. 50.

p. 62   Hemingway, "By God they have bullfights . . ." is from Baker 1981,
            p. 88.

Chapter 6. Becoming the Real Thing

p. 63   Hemingway, "I am getting very fond . . ." is quoted in Baker 1981,
            p. 101.

p. 63 Callaghan, "was willing to be ruthless . . ." is quoted in Baker 1969, p. 121.

p. 64 Hadley Hemingway, "Our hearts are heavy . . ." is quoted in Lynn, p. 223.

p. 64 Hemingway, "It seems in a different . . ." is from White, p. 108.

p. 64 Hemingway, "The Feathercat, Her Book," appears in Hadley Hemingway's copy of *Three Stories and Ten Poems,* Rare Book Reading Room, Library of Congress.

p. 64 Hemingway, "The first matador got the horn . . ." is from E. Hemingway, *in our time,* p. 10.

p. 64 Hemingway, "There was a woman . . ." is from E. Hemingway, *in our time,* p. 11.

p. 65 Grace Hemingway, "mature in judgment" and "You will never know . . ." are in a letter from Grace Hemingway to Ernest Hemingway, December 26, 1923. JFK.

p. 66 MacLeish, "Hemingway, in his loft . . ." is from MacLeish 1978, p. 79.

p. 66 MacLeish, "I've never seen a man . . ." is quoted in Lynn, p. 260.

p. 66 Hemingway, "When I stopped writing . . ." is from E. Hemingway, *Moveable,* p. 76.

p. 66 Pound, "He's an experienced journalist . . ." is quoted in Ford, p. 295.

p. 67 Ford, "I did not read more . . ." is from Ford, p. 323.

p. 67 Dr. Adams [Hemingway], "I don't know, Nick . . ." is from Hemingway, *In Our Time,* p. 21.

p. 67 "a sensitive feeling . . . ," "moments when life is condensed . . . ," and "minute narratives that eliminate . . ." are quoted in Baker 1969, p. 125.

p. 68 Wilson, "profound emotions and complex states . . ." is from Wilson, p. 340.

p. 68 Wilson, "has more artistic dignity . . ." is from Wilson, p. 341.

p. 68 Hemingway, "I wonder what was the matter . . ." is in a letter from Ernest Hemingway to his family, May 7, 1924. LILLY.

p. 68 Beach, "As for Bumby . . ." is from Beach, p. 82.

p. 69 Stewart, "Ernest was somebody . . ." is from Stewart, p. 131.

p. 69 Stewart, "I had shown I could take it . . ." is from Stewart, p. 133.

p. 70 Dos Passos, "had an extraordinary dedication . . ." is from Dos Passos, p. 155.

p. 70 Hemingway, "Every meal time was a great event," is from E. Hemingway, *Moveable,* p. 201.

p. 71   Hemingway, "as natural as the pattern . . ." is from E. Hemingway, *Moveable,* p. 147.

p. 72   Fitzgerald, "He's the real thing," is from Turnbull, p. 167.

p. 72   Stein, "lost generation," is quoted in E. Hemingway, *Moveable,* p. 29.

p. 72   Hemingway, "Made me feel sick," is from Baker 1981, p. 168.

p. 73   Stewart, "One night there was almost . . ." is from Stewart, p. 144.

p. 74   Barnes [Hemingway], "Under the wine I lost . . ." is from E. Hemingway, *The Sun Also Rises,* p. 150.

p. 75   Campbell [Hemingway], "Don't you know you're not . . ." and "What if Brett did sleep . . ." are from E. Hemingway, *Sun Also,* p. 146.

p. 75   Ashley [Hemingway], "Oh, Jake . . .we could have had . . ." is from E. Hemingway, *Sun Also,* p. 251.

p. 75   Hemingway, "It's nice as hell . . . ," "Isn't it nice to think so" and "The End . . . Paris—Sept. 21—1925," are quoted in Baker 1969, p. 155.

Chapter 7. Generations

p. 76   Beach, "I think Hemingway's titles . . ." is from Beach, p. 83.

p. 76   Barnes [Hemingway], "Isn't it pretty to think so?" is from E. Hemingway, *Sun Also,* p. 251.

p. 78   Hemingway, "wading with the water deepening . . ." and "In the swamp fishing . . ." are from E. Hemingway, *In Our Time,* p. 211.

p. 78   Hemingway, "Nick had one good trout . . ." is from E. Hemingway, *In Our Time,* p. 207.

p. 78   "lyricism, aliveness and energy," is quoted in Lynn, p. 306.

p. 78   "lean, pleasing, tough resilience," is quoted in Baker 1969, p. 158.

p. 79   "America's most interesting writer," is quoted in Schevill, p. 611.

p. 79   Anderson, "Bruce Dudley stood near a window . . ." is from Anderson 1925, p. 9.

p. 79   Hemingway, "Yogi Johnson stood looking out . . ." is from E. Hemingway, *The Torrents of Spring,* p. 21.

p. 80   Aiken, "understanding and revelation . . ." is from Aiken, p. 4.

p. 80   Grace Hemingway, "doubtful honor," "one of the filthiest books," and "could not face being present," are in a letter from Grace Hemingway to Ernest Hemingway, December 4, 1926. JFK.

p. 80   Hemingway, "the real inner lives . . ." and "You must remember . . ." are from Baker 1981, p. 243.

p. 80   Clarence E. Hemingway, "I shall trust your future . . . ," "a serious domestic trouble," and "that you and Hadley . . ." are in a letter from Clarence E. Hemingway to Ernest Hemingway, December 13, 1926. JFK.

p. 80   Hemingway, "All things truly wicked . . ." is from E. Hemingway, *Moveable,* p. 210.

p. 82   Hemingway, "I wished I had died . . ." is from E. Hemingway, *Moveable,* p. 210.

p. 82   Hemingway, "the other thing started again," is from E. Hemingway, *Moveable,* p. 211.

p. 82   Hemingway, "I like to think about death . . ." is quoted in Baker 1969, p. 167.

p. 82   Hemingway, "the best and truest . . ." is from Baker 1981, p. 228.

p. 82   [caption] Murphy, "miscast," and "cleanly and sharply," are from Miller, p. 22.

p. 83   Hemingway, "It is the only thing . . ." is from Baker 1981, p. 228.

p. 83   [caption] Hadley [Hemingway] Mowrer, "fell very hard in love with Pauline," is from an undated interview with Hadley Mowrer. JFK.

p. 83   Perkins, "The Sun has risen . . ." is quoted in Baker 1969, p. 182.

p. 84   Hemingway, "They were white in the sun . . ." is from E. Hemingway, *Men Without Women,* p. 50.

p. 84   "theory of omission," is from Oliver, p. 545.

p. 85   Hemingway, "There's nothing wrong with me . . ." is from E. Hemingway, *Men,* p. 55.

p. 85   Hemingway, "shut up like a hermit crab," "was entirely my fault . . ." "I will never stop loving . . . ," and "You cannot know how . . ." are from Baker 1981, pp. 257–59.

p. 85   Parker, "The simple thing he does . . ." is quoted in Lynn, p. 310.

p. 85   Woolf, "The greatest writers lay no stress . . ." is quoted in Lynn, p. 369.

p. 88   "will double in value . . ." is from Ellerbe, unnumbered page.

p. 89   Dos Passos, "Hem always did have a gang . . ." is from Dos Passos, p. 199.

p. 90   Hemingway, "Patrick is like a bull . . . ," "bug house," and "I must write this book . . ." are in a letter from Ernest Hemingway to Waldo Peirce, July 23, 1928. JFK.

Chapter 8. Dangerous Game

p. 92 Hemingway, "My father was a coward . . ." is quoted in Baker 1969,
       p. 609.

p. 93 Henry [Hemingway], "false feeling of soldiering," is from
       E. Hemingway, *Farewell,* p. 17.

p. 93 Henry [Hemingway], "summer lightning," is from E. Hemingway,
       Farewell, p. 3.

p. 94 Henry [Hemingway], "In the column there were . . ." is from
       E. Hemingway, *Farewell,* p. 198.

p. 94 Henry [Hemingway], "I was always embarrassed . . ." is from
       E. Hemingway, *Farewell,* pp.184–85.

p. 96 Perkins, "certain words," is quoted in Lynn, p. 382.

p. 96 Hemingway, "If a word can be printed . . ." is from Baker 1981, p. 297.

p. 96 "blossoming of a most unusual . . ." and "It is brutal . . ." are from
       Butcher, p. 11.

p. 96 "If anything better . . ." is from Cowley, p. 16.

p. 99 Dos Passos, "They thought he was the most . . ." is from Dos Passos,
       p. 205.

p.100 Pauline Hemingway, "I have never seen anyone . . ." is quoted in Baker
       1969, p. 217.

p.101 Hemingway, "cold, serene, and intelligent valor," is from
       E. Hemingway, *Death,* p. 473.

p.101 Hemingway, "When writing a novel . . ." and "People in a novel . . ."
       are from E. Hemingway, *Death,* p. 191.

p.102 Hemingway, "fascinated by death . . ." and "it takes more cojones . . ."
       are from E. Hemingway, *Death,* p. 22.

p.102 Hemingway, "grace under pressure," is quoted in Parker, p. 31.

p.102 Hemingway, "danger only exists . . ." is from E. Hemingway, ed., *Men,*
       p. xxiv.

p.102 Hemingway, "Whatever I had to do . . ." is from E. Hemingway, ed.,
       Men, p. xii.

p.104 Hemingway, "This was the kind . . . ," "to feel the grass . . . ," and "I
       had been quite ill . . ." are from E. Hemingway, *Green Hills of
       Africa,* pp. 51 and 55.

p.105 Hemingway, "the biggest, widest, darkest . . ." is from E. Hemingway,
       Green Hills, p. 291.

p.105 Percival, "have very primitive . . ." and "impossible not to be . . ." are
       quoted in E. Hemingway, *Green Hills,* p. 293.

p.105 Hemingway, "hungry for more of it," is from E. Hemingway, *Green Hills*, p. 73.

p.105 Hemingway, "It was a nothing . . ." is from E. Hemingway, *Complete Short Stories*, p. 291.

p.106 Fadiman, "I can't feel that your stories . . ." is from Fadiman, p. 75.

Chapter 9. "Wonderful . . . Irreplaceable . . . Impossible"

p.107 Hemingway, "at the end of the world," is quoted in Baker 1969, p. 272.

p.107 Hemingway, "Go wherever you want . . ." is quoted in G. Hemingway, p. 25.

p.109 MacLeish, "fed up with the world . . ." is quoted in Baker 1969, p. 262.

p.109 MacLeish, "He was a wonderful . . ." is from Bush, p. 87.

p.110 Dos Passos, "famous author, the great sports . . ." and "We tried to keep him . . ." are from Dos Passos, p. 219.

p.110 Hemingway, "I know that anyone . . ." is from Baker 1981, p. 412.

p.110 Hemingway, "to write an absolutely true . . ." is from E. Hemingway, *Green Hills,* unnumbered page.

p.112 Hemingway, "more dead than I'd seen . . ." is from Baker 1981, p. 421.

p.112 "It used to be pretty exciting . . ." and "He thinks he can write . . ." are quoted in Lynn, p. 426.

p.112 "not exactly a poor book . . ." is from DeVoto, p. 5.

p.113 Wilson, "is certainly his own worst-drawn . . ." is quoted in Lynn, p. 426.

p.113 Hemingway, "It makes me more tolerant . . ." is from Baker 1981, p. 436.

p.113 Hemingway, *"He had seen the world . . ."* is from E. Hemingway, *Complete Short Stories,* p. 49.

p.113 Hemingway, "as wide as all the world . . ." is from E. Hemingway, *Complete Short Stories,* p. 56.

p.114 Hemingway, "a special glamourous race . . ." is from E. Hemingway, *Complete Short Stories,* p. 53.

p.114 Fitzgerald, "it doesn't mean I want . . ." is from Turnbull, p. 311.

p.114 Fitzgerald, "quite as nervously broken . . ." is from Turnbull, p. 543.

p.114 Hemingway, "He was very wealthy . . ." and "His wife had been . . ." are from E. Hemingway, *Complete Short Stories,* p. 18.

p.114 Hemingway, "he felt a sudden white-hot . . ." is from E. Hemingway, *Complete Short Stories,* p. 27.

p.116 Morgan [Hemingway], "One man alone ain't got . . ." is from

E. Hemingway, *To Have and Have Not,* p. 150.

p. 117 Gellhorn, "You are a fine girl . . ." is from Moorehead, p. 47.

p. 118 Hemingway, "Why do they stay? . . ." is from E. Hemingway, *The Spanish Earth,* pp. 45–46.

p. 118 Ivens, "Hemingway liked to accompany me . . ." is quoted in Brian, p. 107.

p. 119 Matthews, "a good man in a pinch," is quoted in Lynn, p. 446.

p. 120 Hemingway, "There is only one form . . ." is from E. Hemingway, "The Writer and War," p. 69.

p. 120 Hemingway, "The Totalitarian fascist states . . ." and "Every time they are beaten . . ." are from E. Hemingway, "Writer," p. 71.

p. 120 Eastman, "an enthusiasm for killing," is from Eastman 1970, p. 96.

p. 120 Eastman, "false hair on the chest," is from Eastman 1970, p. 95.

p. 120 Hemingway, "jumped at me like a woman . . ." is quoted in Baker 1969, p. 317.

p. 120 Gregory Hemingway, "He had brought back . . ." is from G. Hemingway, p. 22.

p. 121 Hemingway, "France is a country . . ." is from White, p. 209.

Chapter 10. Life Is Now

p. 122 "a stupid and foolish book . . ." is from Schwartz, p. 777.

p. 122 "shocking lapses from professional skill," is quoted in Lynn, p. 463.

p. 122 "are to reach a further . . ." is from "All Stories End . . . ," p. 7.

p. 122 Hemingway, "Life is quite complicated" and "not get discouraged . . ." are from Baker 1981, p. 493.

p. 123 Hemingway, "very bad example" is from Baker 1981, p. 493.

p. 124 Donne, "Any man's death diminishes . . ." is from Donne, p. 620.

p. 124 Jordan [Hemingway], "I suppose it is possible . . ." is from E. Hemingway, *For Whom,* p. 166.

p. 124 Jordan [Hemingway], "principle of the fox," is from E. Hemingway, *For Whom,* p. 11.

p. 124 Jordan [Hemingway], "Not time, not happiness . . ." is from E. Hemingway, *For Whom,* p. 168.

p. 125 Jordan [Hemingway], "and that is all . . ." is from E. Hemingway, *For Whom,* p. 169.

p. 126 Jordan [Hemingway], "Thou art me too now . . ." is from E. Hemingway, *For Whom,* p. 464.

p. 126 Jordan [Hemingway], "You've had just as good . . ." is from

E. Hemingway, *For Whom,* p. 467.

p.126 Hemingway, "Anyhow, it is a hell . . ." is from Baker 1981, p. 506.

p.126 "rare and beautiful," and "He has done his finest . . ." are from Sherwood, unnumbered page.

p.126 Fitzgerald, "It's a fine novel . . ." and "to read the whole . . ." are from Turnbull, p. 312.

p.126 John Hemingway, "use the 'f' word," is quoted in Moorehead, p. 44.

p.128 Hemingway, "terraced, gray, bomb-spattered . . ." is from White, p. 335.

p.128 Hemingway, "ragged, torn-clothed," and "they work all day . . ." are from White, p. 338.

p.129 Hemingway, "I have seen much war . . ." is from E. Hemingway, ed., *Men at War,* p. xxvii.

p.132 Welsh, "Above the great, bushy . . ." is from M. Hemingway, p. 94.

p.132 Hemingway, "I don't know you . . ." is from M. Hemingway, p. 95.

p.133 "floating cigar box," is from Frampton, p. 2.

p.133 Hemingway, "like a blast furnace," is from White, p. 342.

p.133 Hemingway, "the finest and bravest . . ." is quoted in Hess, p. 22.

p.133 Lanham, "That is all he wanted . . ." is quoted in J. Stein, p. 2.

p.133 Hemingway, "We have had a tough . . ." and "Small Friend," are from Baker 1981, p. 558.

p.134 Bruce, "was a real expert . . ." is quoted in Baker 1969, p. 411.

p.135 Hemingway, "because there now, below . . ." is from White, p. 383.

p.135 "It was brutal . . ." is from Morello, p. B1.

p.136 Perkins, "Hemingway is through," is quoted in Berg, p. 447.

p.136 Hemingway, "best and most loyal . . ." is from Baker 1981, p. 622.

p.136 Hemingway, "You have given me . . ." is quoted in Tessitore, p.170.

Chapter 11. Out Where No One Can Help

p.139 Faulkner, "His best. . . ." is from Faulkner, p. 55.

p.139 "the best story Hemingway . . ." is quoted in Lynn, p. 565.

p.139 Hemingway, "too far out," is from E. Hemingway, *The Old Man and the Sea,* p. 14.

p.139 Santiago [Hemingway], "But man is not made . . ." is from E. Hemingway, *Old Man,* p. 103.

p.139 "a work of this nature," is quoted in Baker 1969, p. 363.

p.141 Hemingway, "I loved her very much . . ." is from Baker 1981, p. 737.

p.141 Percival, "The whole thing . . ." is quoted in Lynn, p. 570.

p. 142 Hemingway, "in the manner of . . ." is from White, p. 444.

p. 144 Swedish Academy, "For his mastery of the art . . ." is from "The Nobel Prize in Literature 1954," p. 1.

p. 144 Hemingway, "How simple the writing . . ." is from E. Hemingway, "Nobel Prize Speech," p. 14.

p. 145 Gregory Hemingway, "an ideal buttress against . . ." is from G. Hemingway, p. 116.

p. 146 Hemingway, "I act cheerful . . ." is quoted in Lynn, p. 581.

p. 146 Hemingway, "all stories, if continued . . ." is from E. Hemingway, *Death,* p. 122.

p. 149 Rome, "My hope and intention . . ." is in a letter from Howard P. Rome to Mary Hemingway, November 1, 1961. JFK.

p. 149 Mary Hemingway, "Not consciously lying . . ." is from M. Hemingway, p. 503.

p. 149 MacLeish, "Death explains . . ." and "The gun between the teeth . . ." are from MacLeish 1985, p. 482.

Epilogue. Remembering

p. 150 "Few Americans had a greater impact . . ." is from Kennedy, p. 1.

p. 150 "Who will ever forget . . ." is from Thomas, p. 15.

p. 150 "He killed his first wild animals . . ." is from "Upton Sinclair, Homer Croy and Robert Graves Dissent," p. 17.

p. 151 "Hemingway's memoir . . ." is from Milford, p. 10.

SELECTED BIBLIOGRAPHY

Hemingway skis in Switzerland in 1927.

Aiken, Conrad. "Expatriates." *New York Herald Tribune Books,* October 31, 1926, p. 4.

"All Stories End . . ." *Time,* October 18, 1937. Available online. URL: http://www.time.com/time/printout/0,8816,27806,00.html. Downloaded on January 12, 2008.

Anderson, Sherwood. *Dark Laughter.* New York: Boni and Liveright, 1925.

———. *Letters of Sherwood Anderson.* Boston: Little, Brown, 1953.

———. *Winesburg, Ohio.* New York: Dover, 1995.

Baker, Carlos. *Ernest Hemingway: A Life Story.* New York: Scribner's, 1969.

———, ed. *Ernest Hemingway: Selected Letters, 1917–1961.* New York: Scribner's, 1981.

Beach, Sylvia. *Shakespeare and Company.* Lincoln, Neb.: University of Nebraska Press, 1991.

Berg, A. Scott. *Max Perkins, Editor of Genius.* New York: Riverhead Books, 1997.

Brian, Denis. *The True Gen: An Intimate Portrait of Ernest Hemingway by Those Who Knew Him*. New York: Grove Press, 1988.

Bruccoli, Matthew J., ed. *Conversations with Ernest Hemingway*. Jackson, Miss.: University Press of Mississippi, 1986.

———. *Ernest Hemingway, Cub Reporter: Kansas City Star Stories*. Pittsburgh: University of Pittsburgh Press, 1970.

———. *Ernest Hemingway's Apprenticeship: Oak Park, 1916–1917*. Washington, D.C.: NCR Microcard Editions, 1971.

Brumback, Ted. "With Hemingway before 'A Farewell to Arms.'" *Kansas City Star,* December 6, 1939, pp. 1C–2C.

Bush, Warren V., ed. *The Dialogues of Archibald MacLeish and Mark Van Doren*. New York: Dutton, 1964.

Butcher, Fanny. "Here Is Genius, Critic Declares of Hemingway." *Chicago Daily Tribune,* September 28, 1929, p. 11.

Cowley, Malcolm. "Not Yet Demobilized." *New York Herald Tribune Books,* October 6, 1929, pp. 1, 16.

DeVoto, Bernard. "Hemingway in the Valley." *Saturday Review of Literature,* October 26, 1935, p. 5.

Donne, John. "Meditation XVII." *Norton Anthology of English Literature,* 3rd ed. New York: Norton, 1975, pp. 619–20.

Dos Passos, John. *The Best Times: An Informal Memoir*. London: Andre Deutsch, 1968.

Eastman, Max. *Art and the Life of Action, with Other Essays*. Freeport, N.Y.: Books for Libraries Press, 1970.

———. *Great Companions: Critical Memoirs of Some Famous Friends*. New York: Farrar, Straus, 1959.

"Editorial." *Journal of the American Medical Association,* December 28, 1918, p. 2154.

Ellerbe, Christopher H. *Fact, Fantasy, and Fraud: The Florida Boom*. N.p., N.d.

Fadiman, Clifton. "A Letter to Mr. Hemingway." *New Yorker,* October 28, 1933, pp. 74–75.

Fanning, Michael. *France and Sherwood Anderson: Paris Notebook, 1921*. Baton Rouge, La.: Louisiana State University Press, 1976.

Faulkner, William. Untitled review of *The Old Man and the Sea. Shenandoah,* autumn 1952, p. 55.

Fenton, Charles A. *The Apprenticeship of Ernest Hemingway: The Early Years.*

New York: Farrar, Straus, 1954.

Ford, Ford Madox. *It Was the Nightingale.* New York: Octagon Books, 1975.

Frampton, Peter. "LCV(p) Landing Craft." *Second World War Experience Centre.* Available online. URL: http://www.war-experience.org/803flotilla/landing_craft.htm. Downloaded on January 23, 2008.

Guarino, Jean. *Yesterday: A Historical View of Oak Park, Illinois.* Vol. 1: *Prairie Days to World War I.* Oak Park, Ill.: Oak Ridge Press, 2000.

Hemingway, Ernest. *The Complete Short Stories of Ernest Hemingway: The Finca Vigía Edition.* New York: Scribner's, 1987.

———. *Dateline Toronto: The Complete* Toronto Star *Dispatches, 1920–1924,* edited by William White. New York: Scribner's, 1985.

———. *Death in the Afternoon.* New York: Touchstone (Simon & Schuster), 1996.

———. *88 Poems,* edited by Nicholas Gerogiannis. New York: Harcourt Brace Jovanovich, 1979.

———. *A Farewell to Arms.* New York: Scribner Paperback Fiction, 1995.

———. *For Whom the Bell Tolls.* New York: Collier Books, 1987.

———. *Green Hills of Africa.* Norwalk, Conn.: Easton Press, 1990.

———. *in our time.* Paris: Three Mountains Press, 1924.

———. *In Our Time: Stories.* New York: Scribner's, 1958.

———. "Letter to a Young Writer." *Mark Twain Journal,* vol. XI, no. 4 (summer 1962), p. 10.

———. *Men Without Women.* New York: Scribner's, 1997.

———. "Monologue to the Maestro: A High Seas Letter." *Esquire,* vol. IV, no. 4 (October 1935), pp. 21, 174A–175A.

———. *A Moveable Feast.* New York: Touchstone (Simon & Schuster), 1996.

———. "The Nobel Prize Speech." *Mark Twain Journal,* vol. XI, no. 4 (summer 1962), p. 14.

———. *The Old Man and the Sea.* New York: Scribner's, 1952.

———. *The Spanish Earth.* Cleveland: J. B. Savage, 1938.

———. *The Sun Also Rises.* New York: Scribner Paperback Fiction, 1995.

———. *Three Stories and Ten Poems.* Dijon, France: Contact Publishing, 1923.

———. *To Have and Have Not.* New York: Scribner Classics, 1999.

———. *The Torrents of Spring.* London: Jonathan Cape, 1964.

———. "The Writer and War," in *The Writer in a Changing World,* edited by Henry Hart. New York: Equinox Cooperative Press, 1937.

———. ed. *Men at War: The Best War Stories of All Time.* New York: Bramhall

House, 1979.

Hemingway, Gregory H. *Papa: A Personal Memoir*. Boston: Houghton Mifflin, 1976.

Hemingway, Leicester. *My Brother, Ernest Hemingway*. Sarasota, Fla.: Pineapple Press, 1996.

Hemingway, Mary Welsh. *How It Was*. New York: Alfred A. Knopf, 1976.

Hess, John L. "Maj. Gen. Charles Lanham Dies; A Soldier Model for Hemingway." *New York Times,* July 22, 1978, p. 22.

Kennedy, John F. "The President's Tribute." *Mark Twain Journal,* summer 1962, p. 1.

Kert, Bernice. *The Hemingway Women*. New York: Norton, 1983.

Lardner, Ring. *Selected Stories*. New York: Penguin Books, 1997.

Lynn, Kenneth S. *Hemingway*. New York: Fawcett Columbine (Ballantine), 1988.

MacLeish, Archibald. *Collected Poems, 1917–1982*. Boston: Houghton Mifflin, 1985.

———. *Riders on the Earth: Essays and Recollections*. Boston: Houghton Mifflin, 1978.

Maziarka, Cynthia, and Donald Vogel, Jr., eds. *Hemingway at Oak Park High: The High School Writings of Ernest Hemingway, 1916–1917*. Oak Park, Ill.: Oak Park and River Forest High School, 1993.

Milford, Nancy. "The False Memoir." *Washington Post Book World,* February 5, 2006, p. 10.

Miller, Linda Patterson, ed. *Letters from the Lost Generation: Gerald and Sara Murphy and Friends*. Gainesville, Fla.: University Press of Florida, 2002.

Moorehead, Caroline, ed. *Collected Letters of Martha Gellhorn*. New York: Henry Holt, 2006.

Morello, Carol. "Brutal Battle in the Forest." *Washington Post,* May 24, 2004, p. B1.

Nagel, James, ed. *Ernest Hemingway: The Oak Park Legacy*. Tuscaloosa, Ala.: University Press of Alabama, 1996.

"The Nobel Prize in Literature 1954." *Nobelprize.org*. Available online. URL: http://nobelprize.org/nobel_prizes/literature/laureates/1954/. Downloaded on January 27, 2008.

Oliver, Charles M. *Critical Companion to Ernest Hemingway: A Literary Reference to His Life and Work*. New York: Facts On File, 2007.

Parker, Dorothy. "The Artist's Reward." *New Yorker,* November 30, 1929, pp. 28–31.

Reynolds, Michael. *The Young Hemingway*. Oxford, U.K.: B. Blackwell, 1987.

Sanford, Marcelline Hemingway. *At the Hemingways: A Family Portrait*. Boston: Little, Brown, 1962.

Schevill, James. *Sherwood Anderson: His Life and Work*. Denver, Colo.: University of Denver Press, 1951.

Schwartz, Delmore. "Ernest Hemingway's Literary Situation." *Southern Review,* spring 1938, pp. 769–82.

Sherwood, Robert. "The Atlantic Bookshelf." *Atlantic Monthly,* November 1940, unnumbered page.

Stein, Gertrude. *The Autobiography of Alice B. Toklas*. New York: Vintage Books, 1990.

Stein, Jacob A. "General Buck Lanham, Ernest Hemingway, and That Woman in Venice." *Washington Lawyer,* January 2003. Available online. URL: https://www.dcbar.org/for_lawyers/resources/publications/washington_lawyer/january_2003/spectator.cfm. Downloaded on January 21, 2008.

Stewart, Donald Ogden. *By a Stroke of Luck: An Autobiography*. New York: Paddington Press, 1975.

Supreme Command of the Royal Italian Army. *The Battle of the Piave (June 15–23, 1918)*. London: Hodder and Stoughton, n.d.

Tessitore, John. *The Hunt and the Feast: A Life of Ernest Hemingway*. New York: Franklin Watts, 1996.

Thomas, Lowell. "Larger than Life." *Mark Twain Journal,* summer 1962, p. 15.

"The Traveler's Paris of To-Day." *American Review of Reviews,* June 1920, p. 625.

Turnbull, Andrew, ed. *The Letters of F. Scott Fitzgerald*. New York: Charles Scribner's Sons, 1963.

"Upton Sinclair, Homer Croy and Robert Graves Dissent." *Mark Twain Journal,* summer 1962, p. 17.

Walpole, Hugh. *Fortitude*. New York: George H. Duran, 1913.

White, William, ed. *By-Line, Ernest Hemingway: Selected Articles and Dispatches of Four Decades*. New York: Touchstone (Simon & Schuster), 1998.

Wilson, Edmund. "Mr. Hemingway's Dry-Points." *Dial,* October 1924, pp. 340–41.

THE MAJOR WORKS OF ERNEST HEMINGWAY

Patrick, Ernest, and Gregory Hemingway play with cats at Finca Vigía, 1946.

(in order of publication)

Novels

The Torrents of Spring: A Romantic Novel in Honor of the Passing of a Great Race. Scribner's, 1926.

The Sun Also Rises. Scribner's, 1926.

A Farewell to Arms. Scribner's, 1929.

To Have and Have Not. Scribner's, 1937.

For Whom the Bell Tolls. Scribner's, 1940.

Across the River and Into the Trees. Scribner's, 1950.

The Old Man and the Sea. Scribner's, 1952.

Islands in the Stream (Hemingway's novel featuring the artist Thomas Hudson). Scribner's, 1970.*

The Garden of Eden (Hemingway's novel concerning a bisexual love triangle). Scribner's, 1986.*

True at First Light (the first published version of Hemingway's second book about Africa). Scribner's, 1999.*

Under Kilimanjaro (the second published version of Hemingway's second book about Africa). Kent State University Press, 2005.*

Nonfiction

Death in the Afternoon. Scribner's, 1932.

Green Hills of Africa. Scribner's, 1935.

A Moveable Feast (Hemingway's memoir of his years in Paris). Scribner's, 1964.*

The Dangerous Summer (Hemingway's account of the summer 1959 bullfighting season in Spain). Scribner's, 1985.*

Short Stories, Poetry, and Drama

Three Stories and Ten Poems. Contact Publishing, 1923.

in our time. Three Mountains Press, 1924.

In Our Time: Stories. Boni and Liveright, 1925.

Men Without Women. Scribner's, 1927.

Winner Take Nothing. Scribner's, 1933.

The Fifth Column and the First Forty-Nine Stories. Scribner's, 1938.

The Fifth Column and Four Stories of the Spanish Civil War. Scribner's, 1969.*

88 Poems. Harcourt Brace Jovanovich, 1979.*

The Complete Short Stories of Ernest Hemingway: The Finca Vigía Edition. Scribner's, 1987.*

*Works followed by an asterisk were published after Hemingway's death. These books were edited, often substantially, by Mary Hemingway, Patrick Hemingway, and others.

PICTURE CREDITS

INDEX

Note: Page numbers in **bold** type refer to illustrations.